Health Care Insurance Reform in the United States

A Market Approach With Application from the Federal Republic of Germany

Frankie Palmer Albritton, Jr., Ph.D.

UNIVERSITY PRESS OF AMERICA

Lanham • New York • London

University Press of America®, Inc.
4720 Boston Way
Lanham, Maryland 20706

3 Henrietta Street
London WC2E 8LU England

Printed in the United States of America
British Cataloging in Publication Information Available

Library of Congress Cataloging-in-Publication Data

Albritton , Jr., Frankie Palmer, 1961–
Health care insurance reform in the United States : a market approach with application from the Federal Republic of Germany / by Frankie Palmer Albritton, Jr.
p. cm.
Includes bibliographical references and index.
1. Insurance, Health—United States. 2. Insurance, Health—Germany. 3. Medical care, Cost of—United States. 4. Medical care, Cost of—Germany. I. Title.
HG9396.A617 1992 368.3'82'00973—dc20 92–31546
CIP

ISBN 0–8191–8896–4 (cloth : alk. paper)

The paper used in this publication meets the minimum requirements of American National Standard for Information Sciences—Permanence of Paper for Printed Library Materials, ANSI Z39.48–1984.

To Angela, for her devotion and support.

TABLE OF CONTENTS

CHAPTER FIVE

LIST OF TABLES AND FIGURES

Tables

Figures

PREFACE

Almost forty million United States citizens do not have access to health care insurance. Many of these are full-time employees or the dependents of full-time employees. This situation is both inefficient and inequitable.

Many of the participants in the health care market, namely physicians and private insurance companies, do not want to see a change in the current market-based health insurance system, citing the ability of a competitive market, free from government intervention, to efficiently allocate resources.

The purpose of this book is twofold. The first is to use economic analysis to show the insufficiency and inequity caused by relying upon the competitive market to provide health care insurance, a situation that leads to market failure and the need for government intervention. The second purpose is to propose a model which deals with this market failure.

The health care insurance system in the Federal Republic of Germany, given its market-based system of care providers and its success at providing its citizens with quality medical care while containing cost, will be used as a basis upon which to propose a model to reform the health care insurance system in the United States.

CHAPTER ONE

A State of Crisis

It may be surprising to note that the United States already has a national health system. It lacks cohesion, it is the subject of attack from all sides, and it is inefficient and inequitable. It consists of federal, state and private players interacting in a confusing and expensive effort (twelve percent of gross national product) to provide U.S. citizens with health care. It has led to huge expenditures that, in some cases, if treatment were given at an earlier stage, would have led to a smaller expenditure with better results.

According to Donald Riegle, a member of the United States Congress, about thirty-seven million Americans have no health insurance at any given time and as many as sixty million may be without insurance during the year. The most astounding fact about these numbers is that many of these people without medical insurance are workers (and their children) with full-time jobs. Many of these workers are employed by small companies that have been forced out of the market for health insurance by the extremely expensive premiums. This large group of U.S. citizens may have access to health care, but a third party with no relationship to the user of the health care may be forced to pay the bill.[1]

The question, however, that must be asked is whether the above situation leads to the most efficient use of resources. The costs to administer such a system lacking coordination are great, as pointed out by Mr. Lynn Etheridge, an independent health care consultant, in testimony before the Committee of Labor and Human Resources of the United States Senate on hearings on the Basic Health Benefits for All American Act. The administrative costs of managing the fragmented market for health insurance is between twenty-five to forty percent of the premiums for small companies and the total administrative costs amount to one hundred billion dollars of the five hundred billion dollars spent in the United States on health care. The opportunity for savings in this area alone is tremendous. [2]

Passing the Buck

The large number of U.S. citizens who go without health insurance and still require medical care are treated at the expense of those who do have insurance because the medical establishment treating these patients must recover the cost of the treatment. These costs are added to the health care bills of companies which in turn hurts the productivity of many firms in comparison to their international competition. In 1988, unpaid hospital bills totaled more than eight billion dollars, up ten percent from the previous year. This necessitates cost-shifting if no state or federal office will pick up the bill, if for example, the worker earned above the level where public assistance could have been given. New Jersey, for example adds a thirteen percent surcharge to each hospital bill to make up for lost revenues from unpaid bills.[3]

Many U.S. companies face huge annual health care bills which do hurt their international competitiveness. In the U.S. automobile industry in 1989, General Motor paid approximately three billion dollars in health care costs, Ford 813 million dollars, and Chrysler 684 million dollars. This, for example, adds seven dollars per hour to Chrysler's labor bill.[4] This hurts Chrysler's competitiveness in relation to a foreign competitor whose workers' health care is paid for by taxes or through a more evenly shared burden within society.

Small But Expensive

The full and part-time workers who are employed by for profit companies that do not have health insurance for their workers are victims of a system that has put health insurance out of the reach of many small businesses. Insurance companies have been forced by decreasing profit margins, due to the spiraling medical bills, to treat each small business as an individual risk and not as part of the population of businesses in a geographic region. This has led to the expensive premiums for small businesses for each worker they employ, with the assumption that the small business can even get an insurance company to offer them insurance. This has led to only half of the companies with fewer than one hundred workers, employing one-third of the U.S. work force, to offer health insurance to their workers. Many companies are forced to drop the insurance they have because after one incident of illness with one of their employees, the insurance company either doubles or triples the premium or drops the coverage. To be able to afford the premiums, many are forced to ask their employees to pay for more of the cost of providing coverage. According to Hewett Associates, a benefits-consulting firm, in 1984 thirty-seven percent of large employers paid the full premium for their employees. In 1988, this was down to twenty-four percent. During this time-period, the percentage of firms that paid all hospital room and board charges for their workers dropped from fifty-three percent to twenty-nine percent.[6]

Insurance companies often refuse to take on companies who have employees with current sickness claims. When a company is trying to get insurance, the insurance representative will look at each employee's health history in small firms and if there is a history of one of the "big five" - cancer, diabetes, heart problems, aids or even pregnancy, the insurance company will often refuse coverage. This has led to many U.S. citizens becoming "hostages" of their current employers if the current employer has a good health insurance program. For instance, a secretary for a small accounting firm in Texas has a child who was born with an immune deficiency disease that leaves the child susceptible to infections. Every four to five weeks, an infusion of antibodies is needed which costs about 2,400 dollars. The cost to the firm for insurance coverage has risen sharply. She has been under pressure to leave her job so that the premiums for the firm's employees can be reduced. She knows in all probability that if she leaves her job, she will never again get the coverage for her daughter, coverage that means the difference between life and death.[7]

Many of the employees not covered by their employers and the self-employed purchase private, individual health insurance. These policies differ in what is covered and of course, how expensive they are. It will depend on age, sex, medical history, etc. Assuming that one can find a reasonable priced policy, one must stay healthy in order for the price of the policy to remain reasonable. For example, a worker in California took out a policy in 1985 that cost him 912 dollars a year and had a one hundred dollar annual deductible. By 1989, the policy had increased in cost to 3,600 dollars. After a knee injury and surgery, his policy increased to 6,900 dollars.[8]

In addition to the problems of lack of insurance and expensive premiums, there is the problem of employees and the self-employed having inadequate insurance. Many have very high deductibles, which make the employee pay for the first several hundred dollars of medical expenses each year. This may dissuade many from seeking the care in a stage where appropriate care could have simply and inexpensively cured the condition. For instance, a newly-hired Nevada casino worker from Canada noticed a mole growth on his chest but he delayed getting the mole examined because his employer's insurance did not cover workers in their first three months of employment and previous medical problems, a common circumstance. After several months of delay, a doctor was consulted and advanced cancer was diagnosed. After paying for his initial medical treatment with bad checks, the worker finally went back to Canada, where as a Canadian citizen, he was eligible for free medical care. Since the cancer was in such an advanced stage, the worker could not be saved and died, leaving two young children.

The above circumstances lead to many expectant mothers going without maternity care, which results in higher numbers of premature babies and thousands of dollars of care being paid for by public sources or being added onto the bills of employers with health insurance. In addition, it is estimated that 7,500 minority deaths per year could be avoided through improved preventive health care. For instance, tuberculosis can be treated in the early stages for as little as twenty cents per day.[9]

Call for a National Health Insurance System

Given the widespread nature of this problem, the calls for a national health system that allows more access to insurance coverage come from many sources. It is in the interest of business to somehow decrease the expenditures on health care while not decreasing the benefits offered to employees. The introduction of such a system in the United States would not take the form of the public provision of health as in England with its National Health Service and the financing of the system with tax dollars given the budget constraints the United States government currently faces.

The American Federation of Labor and the Congress of Industrial Organizations (AFL-CIO), has published a series of pamphlets entitled, "National Health Care Reform," which advocate a more centralized solution to solving the crisis resulting from rising health care costs and the large number of uninsured workers. Their members are increasingly bearing the brunt of cost-cutting reforms that businesses are undertaking to get a handle on the rising cost of medical care. For instance, recent changes in the health care policies of three large companies include Allied Signal Corporation making their employees pay all their medical bills up to one percent of salary, J.C. Penny covering families only when the employee is the principal earner in the family, and Armstrong Industries stopping the practice of promising health care benefits to employees when they retire.[10]

The AFL-CIO has proposed guidelines that it thinks should be followed in any proposal for a national health insurance system. These include: Guaranteed quality health care for all Americans under federal law with the availability of affordable insurance with comprehensive coverage, and a system efficient in containing health care cost increases which takes advantage of the current strengths of the present system.[11]

Many members of the United States Congress have begun to call for reforms in the health care system and even for reforms in health insurance availability. This is not surprising, since they realize the necessity of keeping members of Congress healthy as is shown by the health benefits that members of Congress, who already earn 123,00 dollars a year, are entitled to. These include low cost premiums, the right to coverage for life for the member of Congress and his family for as long as the member lives, and the right of access to a large medical clinic, with all the amenities, free of charge. The bill for the clinic alone comes to two million dollars a year.[12]

The Proposal

The above description of some of the problems facing the U.S. health care system illustrates some of the failures of the current system which are primarily efficiency and equity. The United State spends twelve percent of its gross national product on health, more than any other country in terms of both total amount spent and as a percentage of gross national product. The United States is, however, the only major industrialized country not to have a system of national health insurance. This paper will be an attempt to explain the current system and point out its faults and give recommendations to address the questions of efficiency and equity.

The system of health care insurance in the Federal Republic of Germany will be used as a comparison to show that efficiency and equity can be combined since the Federal Republic of Germany spends only eight percent of its gross national product on health care, but it has ninety-seven percent of its population covered by statutory health insurance coverage.[13]

The above success is possible through employer provided mandated insurance and insurance for the unemployed and the poor. This is accomplished through a system of private providers, as in the United States, whose primary source of remuneration are through the sickness funds that also perform a monitoring function on the charges by doctors and in turn are regulated by the government. Thus, this is a system that could be used as model in the United States through the enactment of laws mandating the coverage of employees and the unemployed and the establishment of similar insurance organizations that treat the population of workers from individual companies as members of a larger group. This would be a system capable of taking advantage of the insurance principle of the law of large numbers to bring down the insurance premiums that are charged to individual members of the insurance pool. This would solve the problem of the large number of uninsured people in the United States while incorporating the existing system of delivery and financing of health care in the United States.

The next chapter of this paper will deal with the economics of health care markets, illustrating the need for a national health insurance system such as the one in Germany. This economic analysis is critical as many doubt the need for government intervention in a system that leads the world in the advancement of medicine. The efficiency of the market is cited as the best way to allocate scarce resources, and a part of the economy that is responsible for the creation of health while producing many jobs and an export surplus of eleven billion dollars in 1990, should not be interfered with.[14]

After the second chapter, the health care insurance markets, first in the United States and then in the Federal Republic of Germany, will be illustrated. From these illustrations, it will be possible to make recommendations to enable the formulation of a health insurance system that will merge the positive aspects of both systems to come up with an efficient, equitable and workable health care insurance system for the United States.

Chapter One Notes

[1]Tom Price, "Uninsured Risk Health Care for All, Panel Told," *Dayton Daily News*, (24 July 1990), 12 B.

[2]U.S. Congress Senate. Committee on Labor and Human Resources, *Basic Health Care for All Americans Act*, 101st Congress, (May and June 1989), 272.

[3]"The Crisis in Health Insurance," *Consumer Reports*, (August 1990), 534.

[4]"Chrysler Proposes Novel Health Plan," *The Stars and Stripes*, (22 July 1990), 3.

[5]"The Crisis in Health Insurance," *Consumer Reports*, (August 1990), 534.

[6]Ibid., 537.

[7]Ibid., 536.

[8]Ibid., 535.

[9]"Minority Health Care," Report from proceeding of the 1991 National Medical Association Conference, *USA Today*, (31 July 1991), 7B.

[10]National Health Care Reform: *Launching the Corporate Campaign*, (AFL-CIO, 1989), 1.

[11]Ibid., 4.

[12] Frank Lalli, "There's a Doctor in the House," *Money*, (July 1991), 5.

[13]Bengt Jönsson, "What Can Americans Learn from Europeans," in *Health Care Systems in Transition: The Search for Efficiency*, (Paris: OECD, 1990), 88.

[14] Kevin Anderson, "Health Spending Pumps USA with Jobs, Growth," *USA Today*, (7 May 1991), 10B.

CHAPTER TWO

The Economics of Health Care

In testimony before the Committee of Labor and Human Resources, in debate on the merits of the Basic Health Care Bill for All Americans, Chairman Edward Kennedy, a U.S. Senator from Massachusetts, asked Mr. Angelo Mendez how he decided to take his children to the hospital when they were sick. Mr. Mendez was recently idled from his job at Kaiser Aluminum where his family had health insurance benefits. His wife worked for a building cleaning company twenty-five hours a week for under five dollars an hour. Mr. Mendez was asked, "when you hear your children either coughing or feeling bad, do you make in your own mind sort of an assessment whether that child is fifty dollars or seventy-five dollars or one-hundred dollars sick?" Mr. Mendez answered that he does, and he had to refrain from taking his children to the doctor recently when they all had come down with a severe ear infection and cold during the harsh Denver winter. Mr. Mendez also caught the cold and had to miss several days from his temporary job. In addition, they are currently paying a six thousand dollar hospital bill for the delivery of their daughter. The bill will be paid off over the next six years at seventy-five dollars a month.[1]

Efficiency and Equity of Competitive Markets

Mr. Mendez, who has no medical training, must make a judgement on how sick his children were and whether it was worth it to take them to a doctor based on the expected cost of the visit. In effect, he was being asked to evaluate his benefit from the visit to the doctor versus the cost. At this point, economic theory of marginal analysis predicts that if Mr. Mendez values the medical services he will receive at one hundred dollars, he will purchase the service as long as it costs him no more than one hundred dollars. This transaction will not alter his "wealth." Indeed, if the services cost him less than one hundred dollars a month, he will be adding to his overall "wealth" by the difference between his estimated benefit and the cost of the services received. However, the correct level of services will be demanded by Mr. Mendez only if he values the services he is receiving at the correct cost and the correct level of benefit to him.

By taking his children to the doctor, Mr. Mendez may know the fee for the office visit, but he is unable to predict, given his limited medical knowledge, the total cost that the visit might entail since the doctor may perform expensive procedures and order expensive tests. In addition, Mr. Mendez does not have the medical training to value this visit to the doctor since by putting the visit off, the condition of his children might worsen and his total cost could increase. He cannot then, put an accurate value on the visit to the doctor.

At this point, a major point of divergence occurs between the relationship of providers and consumers in the medical market and the normal supply and demand relationship in theoretical competitive markets for goods not as complicated as medical services. Most markets in the United States are judged upon how competitive the suppliers of the product are. Competitive market theory simply implies that the more suppliers of a product, the better off the consumer is as he will have the maximum choice at the lowest price.

The above situation can be simply illustrated when a comparison is done using a simple agricultural product such as apples. If there are many sellers of apples in a market square, the consumer could easily compare price and quality of the apples of different sellers and thus make an easy evaluation of where his best buy would occur, since the apples of the various seller would not vary significantly, if at all, and the major consideration would be price. He would bargain with the various sellers of apples to get the lowest price possible. Now if there was only one seller of apples at the market (monopoly) or if each seller sold a unique brand of apple, the process of selection would be immensely more difficult. The buyer would inevitably pay more for each apple based upon the real or imagined difference in quality of each seller's apples, or in the case of monopoly, pay the asked price for apples as long as it was within his ability to do so.

Competitive Health Care Markets

Given the benefits of a competitive market, it is no wonder that if such a market for medical services could be promoted, it would be beneficial to the consumer of medical services, leading to an abundant number of providers and low costs. The primary question then is whether such a competitive market can be promoted successfully in the market for medical services? To answer this question, the standard tenets of competitive theory must be examined.

Standard competitive market theory requires that:

1. There be many suppliers of the commodity (suppliers having little control over price)
2. There is easy entry and exit in the market for suppliers
3. The product or service be homogeneous (products or services are similar)
4. Consumers have adequate information about prices in order to make the correct decisions (lack of price distortions)

In the health care market in the United States, only the first of these requirements is partially fulfilled, namely that there are many suppliers, but it is questionable as to whether they actually compete with each other, which is the benefit of having many suppliers. Since none of these requirements are completely met, it cannot be expected that the health care market will operate as a competitive market because the services are dissimilar, medical schools and the professional organizations limit entry, and consumers are not faced with the full price of the medical services because of the existence of insurance, nor do they accurately value the services. Given these facts, the consumer does not benefit from a truly competitive market which would allow the consumer the widest possible selection at the most competitive prices.

Many Suppliers and Easy Exit and Entry

The very fact that doctors belong to common self-governing bodies, consult with one another and share hospital facilities contradicts the notion that the suppliers of the service do act as independent suppliers of the services. Adam Smith, the "father of economics" and the champion of competitive markets, made this observation and noted it in his book, *The Wealth of Nations*, first published in 1776, which sums up the situation that can occur in medical markets with these words, "People of the same trade seldom meet together, even for merriment and diversion, but the conversation ends in a conspiracy against the public, or in some contrivance to raise prices."[2] This lack of perfect information has long led government to intervene in medical markets in the licensing of doctors and in the prescription of drugs.[3]

Since the end of the Second World War, the United States has encouraged the increase in the supply of medical professionals, especially physicians. Again, according to competitive theory, this should lead to the lowering of the price for physician services as the supply increased and they were forced to compete for patients. Unfortunately, this has not been the case. In 1989, physicians on the average made 155,800 dollars a year after expenses such as malpractice insurance. This translates into an annual increase in income twenty percent higher than the average wage earner in the United States in the period from 1981 to 1989. On average, surgeons made 220,500 dollars in 1989. This is despite the fact that the number of physicians rose 130 percent from 1960 to 1989, while the population of the United States grew by only thirty-six percent.[4]

Homogenous Products and Adequate Information

The ability of physicians to increase their income is a result of the physician being the key component of the health care system. Few tests are conducted or procedures undertaken without the orders of a physician. It should come as no surprise that California has both the highest per capita number of neurosurgeries and neurosurgeons. In Canada, this ability to create demand for surgeries has led to the strict control of the in-migration of surgeons after it was established that each new physician created new expenditures of 300,000 dollars annually.[5]

Considering the situation of Mr. Mendez, he has no idea how serious the condition of his children could become since he has no medical training and he cannot evaluate the value of the medical services available in terms of what services exist or to the long term consequences of not using the services. He does not take his children to the doctor because he does not have insurance. A situation that could be treated with one visit to a doctor and fifty dollars of medicine could turn into a life threatening situation and major medical expenses. This avoidance of small medical expenses due to the ignorance of the possible results of not seeking care are well documented in the case of neo-natal care. The United States spends 2.5 billion dollars annually to care for low birth weight children, many of whose complications could have been avoided with appropriate pre-natal care which averages four hundred to six hundred dollars per pregnancy. A day in a neo-natal intensive care unit costs 1,000 to 1,500 dollars and the usual stay in a hospital lasts eight to ten days and can cost up to 500,000 dollars.[6]

In addition to the consumer not being able to evaluate his need for the services because of his lack of information about a very complex service (versus the situation with agricultural products, an example of a homogeneous product and the common example used to illustrate competitive markets), the consumer has difficulty in determining the quality of the services he is receiving. The products are not homogeneous with one doctor possibly charging more than another with the consumer not knowing what he may be getting for the extra fee, if indeed he is getting anything. He also lacks the information to judge which procedures are necessary from those which are not. This command over information leaves the supply of medical services far outside the realm of the theory of competitive markets.

The United States has left the solution of its health care needs to a great extent to market forces. However, the above examples of imperfect information and imperfect competition in health care markets along with the inability of many to get affordable health insurance coverage, are good reasons for government intervention because of market failure.

Government Intervention in the Health Care Market

When considering whether government intervention is appropriate in any market, there are many considerations. Important among these are:

1. Need for the government intervention
2. Market failure addressed by the government intervention
3. Markets affected by government intervention
4. Form of government intervention with given political environment

The first chapter and the beginning of this chapter have illustrated the inability of the medical market to perform as a competitive market with the resulting market failure in the provision of affordable health benefits to many United States citizens, with the subsequent inefficiencies that result (such as the making of uninformed decisions in the case of Mr. Mendez), and the wasting of resources through higher than necessary prices.

To deal with the market failure and its resulting inefficiencies, a program that would enable the vast majority of U.S. citizens to have access to medical services needs to be implemented. The primary market failure that such a program will deal with is the inability of many U.S. citizens to obtain health insurance. Under a proposal based on the experience in Germany, the inability of U.S. citizens to obtain health care insurance will be solved and this will go a long way in dealing with the second issue, cost control.

Market Failure Addressed by Government Intervention

While Mr. Mendez has no health insurance because of his unemployed status, a more perplexing problem lies with the failure of the market based system to provide health insurance to full-time workers. For a workforce to reach its maximum productivity, it must be, among other things, skilled, motivated, well-managed and healthy. To experience productivity gains, workers must be counted on to be at work. Workers who do not get adequate medical care may not be able to perform at their peak or if they do get to the point where they are so sick they have to go to a hospital, the recovery period may be longer than if they had gotten earlier treatment. For example, eight percent of people with diabetes in the United States have no insurance. This can be easily understood when combined with the situation that most health insurance is unavailable to those with pre-existing conditions, especially those among the previously mentioned "big five."

One example of the detrimental effects that the lack of a health insurance market available to all can cause can be seen in the situation of a self-employed plumber with diabetes, who cannot get health insurance until he becomes disabled and qualifies for social security protection. At this point, society will have lost the services of a productive member of society and in the end will pay much more to support this disabled worker than it would have cost to have provided him with insurance and proper care.[7]

Without the change in the current structure of the U.S. health care system, the situation will worsen as the economy moves closer to a predominately service oriented economy. In a study done in 1977 by the National Medical Care Expenditure Survey, it was found that the likelihood that a worker would have access to employer sponsored health care depended upon such factors as the type of industry, unionization status, full or part-time status, and geographic region. For instance, there has been a marked shift away from manufacturing jobs in the United States to those in service industries. Table 2.1 illustrates this trend away from the manufacturing based jobs to service industries, with service industries having a lower likelihood of offering health insurance plans

Table 2.1 Distribution of Employment* by Industry, United States, 1977 and 1984

Industry	1977 (%)	1984 (%)
Mining	1.0	1.0
Construction	4.6	4.7
Manufacturing	23.9	20.5
Transportation & Public Utilities	5.7	5.5
Trade	22.5	23.4
Finance, Insurance & Real Estate	5.4	6.0
Services	18.6	22.0
Government	18.3	16.9
Total	100.0	100.0

Source: *Monthly Labor Review*, volume 108 (November 1985), table 9. *Nonagricultural

to its workers. The U.S. Bureau of Labor and Statistics forecasts that this trend away from manufacturing-based jobs will continue through 1995.[8]

In addition to the move towards service industries and the related lack of provision of health benefits, the percentage of workers who are represented by unions has also been decreasing. Between 1961 and 1984, the percentage of workers employed by unionized firms dropped from seventy-three percent to fifty-one percent, with ninety-seven percent of firms with some union representation offering health insurance plans and only 80.7 percent of service-oriented firms offering coverage in 1977.[9]

Part-time workers are much less likely to be covered under health insurance plans than full-time workers. This can be attributed to the emphasis business in the U.S. has placed on flexibility and the ability to decrease employment in slow economic periods. This has led to more use of temporary workers and to part-time workers, two groups that are much less likely to be offered health insurance.[10]

The movement of industry from the "Rust Belt" to the "Sun Belt," of the South, has also led to fewer workers being offered health insurance. In 1984, sixty-nine percent of production workers in the Midwest were covered by collective bargaining agreements with only thirty-two percent of manufacturing workers covered in the South, with the resultant lower levels of health insurance coverage in nonunionized firms.[11]

The above trends clearly point to a changing work environment in the United States, one where workers move into industries that typically do not offer lucrative benefit packages, among which is the right to health insurance. This is another indication of the inability of the market to solve the problem of the lack of access to health benefits and the resulting inefficiencies.

Markets Affected by Government Intervention

Given the market's failure, as shown by as many as thirty-seven million people in the United States, many of these full-time workers, who do not have health insurance, there is a need for government intervention, since many of these workers are not eligible for public assistance because they do work. The form of intervention by government in the health care market to deal with this market failure is either direct provision of government financed or subsidized insurance or mandated insurance benefits paid primarily by the employer. These two methods can only be adequately explored after looking at the nature of insurance in the United States, consumer behavior, the history of the government provided or mandated insurance and comparisons with countries that provide insurance coverage or mandate benefits for their citizens.

Insurance. Naturally, the basic objective of any insurance is to reduce the risk that any individual faces and shift this risk to those more willing and able to bear the risk. When insurance companies offer insurance, they normally want to offer the insurance to as large a group as possible, using statistics to approximate how many in the group will be affected and then charging premiums to the group to cover the expected claims and administrative costs. Those in the group that experience predictable losses will be assisted with their burden through the insurance provided by other members of the group.

One recent development in the insurance industry in the United States is the degree of competition between insurance firms for the pool of healthy insureds, especially those that do not have one of the "big five." In 1981, health insurance profits for insurance companies were high, but by 1987, three billion dollars had been lost. [12] Overall demand for private health insurance has been in a steep decline in the 1980's. In addition, many large companies are starting to self-insure. Well over half the employer market now self-insures compared to five percent in the 1970's. Therefore, insurance companies are going after the small employer market. They, however, instead of competing through price competition, are competing in their underwriting practices, using a method called experience-rating, which precludes the insuring of anyone with a prior or current illness. This is because twenty percent of the population with the highest health expenses accounts for eighty percent of national spending on health care, with the top five percent accounting for fifty percent, or 250 billion dollars.[13]

The above means that those employees and citizens who do have medical problems will be excluded from coverage because they are in fact a bad risk. This is inefficient as under the classical economic definition of efficiency, one situation is more efficient than another when someone or a group is made better off than before without another person or group being made worse off. The group which can be offered insurance at a lower price because of the exclusion of the poor risks is better off because of the lower price, but the group which now must go without the insurance is much worse off. As pointed out earlier, however, a member of the group offered the insurance might suffer an illness once insurance coverage is obtained and then become a victim of experience-rating and see premiums for the insurance go up, sometimes beyond the point that the person can afford. In fact this procedure by the private health care insurance market has led to premiums where only those who expect to have illness will be willing to pay the high cost of private health insurance, thus driving up even further the costs of obtaining insurance for those willing to pay the price. For instance, if one's valuation of the worth of medical insurance is two hundred dollars per month, one will pay up to and including that amount to purchase the insurance. If that insurance costs more than the perceived benefit of two hundred dollars, the insurance will not be purchased leaving only those in the pool who value the insurance coverage at or more than its cost. These are usually people who expect to suffer an illness and are the last people that the insurance company wants to insure.

Experience-rating is a vicious circle for the profit seeking insurance company. The only members of society who will be willing on average to purchase insurance are those who expect illness, namely the elderly and those who expect illness or can conceal one from the insurance company.

Consumer Behavior. It is necessary at this point to illustrate the effects of health insurance on consumer behavior and explore two arguments often used to justify the limited provision of health insurance by private industry under market forces versus the liberal benefits under government-provided or mandated health insurance. This can be broken down into consumption changes induced by the existence of health insurance and the problem of moral hazard.

Health insurance lowers the cost of medical care to consumers and perhaps lowers it below the optimum level of efficiency for society. For instance, if the consumer pays only twenty percent of the cost of medical services he receives and the other eighty percent is paid for by the insurance company, then a service that a consumer receives which actually costs two hundred dollars, will cost with insurance only forty dollars. As can be seen from figure 2.1, the consumer will use Q_1 of services where on the surface, Q_0 would be a more efficient point where the consumer pays all of the costs of the medical services, thus correctly equating his marginal, or additional cost of the services received, with his marginal benefit, or the benefit of the additional services received. As, however, was shown with the case of Mr. Mendez in his

Figure 2.1 Insurance and Demand for Medical Services

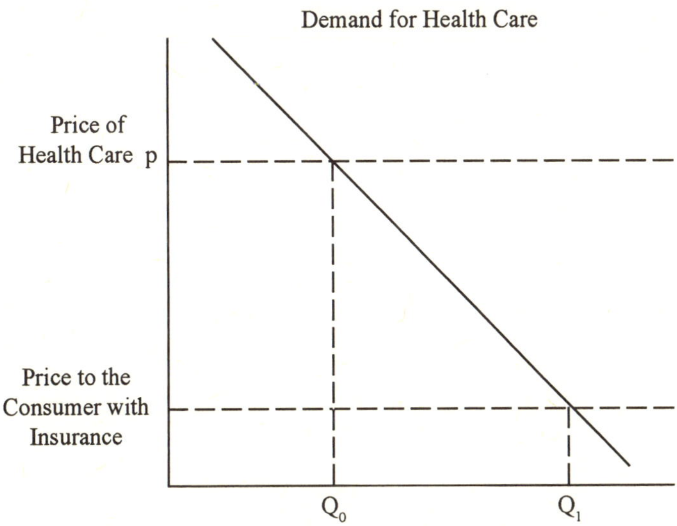

testimony before the U.S. Congress, the normal consumer of health services has great difficulty in judging his correct benefit from health services, leading to a possible underusage and not overusage of services, with increased costs to the individual and society.

If insurance is such a good bargain to the consumer, as illustrated in the above example, then more consumers would purchase insurance as their income increased, thus leading to more health care expenditures. In fact, even though there have been substantial increases in income and spending on health care in some countries, these were not accompanied by the corresponding increases in spending on health insurance. A good example of this is the United States, where the number of people with health insurance is decreasing while the costs of health care outpaces the increase in inflation in the general economy.[14] Therefore, the explanation for the increased portion of gross national product that is consumed by health care cannot be blamed on the increased amount of insurance coverage in the economy.

The second problem with the use of insurance, moral hazard, deals with the results of individuals undertaking risks that they would not, without insurance, be willing to undertake. A good example of this is the use of tobacco. This theory suggests that smokers are more willing to smoke because they have insurance to cover any illness that is a result of smoking. An argument that undermines this theory is that it is in the interests of the insurance companies to educate the consumer as to the dangers of smoking, thus leading to the decreased use of tobacco and other detrimental actions and not more detrimental actions because of insurance.

While the arguments concerning overconsumption of health care because of insurance and moral hazard may or may not be valid, the inefficiencies and inequities of allowing large segments of the population to go without adequate medical care because of lack of medical insurance cannot be disputed. At this point, it may be useful to examine the history of government-provided or mandated national health insurance, looking at the reasons for its provision and the success it has enjoyed where it has been introduced.

<u>History of Government-Provided or Mandated Insurance</u>. The first comprehensive form of national health insurance occurred in 1883 in Germany under Otto von Bismarck, the first chancellor of a united Germany. The system was one of compulsory national health care insurance designed to bind the

citizens to the newly formed country. Since then, all European countries have introduced various forms of national health insurance including the National Health Service in Great Britain, which is a case where the government owns the majority of the health care facilities and employs the majority of the health care professionals, predominantly financed through general tax revenues.

A question that should be asked in the face of the overwhelming support that European countries give national health insurance, is whether there are positive benefits to society, and not just to the individual, when the government provides or mandates health insurance.

There is clear indication of a benefit to society when the government provision of health care leads to the control or even the eradication of communicable diseases. The positive effect of this type of government intervention is, of course, clearly evident. This prevention of disease is a good example of a public good, or a good that when the government provides it, many benefit who do not pay for the protection or even pay taxes. When a good can be defined as a public good, it has passed an economic litmus test, which deems government intervention as necessary. In fact, it would be impossible to charge for this protection of those not infected, and by vaccinating the population free of charge, those who are not vaccinated also benefit.

In the United States, for instance, low income families can have their children vaccinated against Measles free of charge. There have, however, been cutbacks in the budgets of programs that provide these services, and as a result, the death rate among children from Measles is the highest it has been in twenty years.[15] A private entity could not justify providing this service as the revenues could not cover the expense and too little of the good in question would be provided. Defense is also another example of a public good. To illustrate, when defense is provided to a country, it is impossible to exclude anyone who lives in the country from this protection, whether or not the person pays the taxes for the protection. In addition, when new people move into the country, the overall security provided by the defense of the country is not reduced by these additions to the population.

While most health care cannot be classified as pure public goods, some less obvious benefits, however, of the government provision of health insurance are pointed out in Victor Fuch's book, *The Health Economy.* It is pointed out that there is a satisfaction received when the government provides health care to those unable to purchase health insurance. This is closely linked to the European view that access to basic health care is a right even though most health care does not fit the criteria of a public good.

Another argument in favor of the government provision of health care or the mandating of insurance benefits is the feeling that the consumption of medical care is beyond the control of individual citizens. Poor health strikes randomly among the population (not considering the action of individuals that negatively affect their health), sometimes causing radical changes in wealth. Government in the United States has as a priority the control of inflation primarily because of its power to randomly redistribute wealth, especially from those on fixed incomes. Why then should government not take into consideration the random distributive effects of ill health? In fact, the U.S. tax code does take this into consideration, giving tax deductions to those whose medical costs reach beyond a certain percentage of income, namely 7.5 percent. This, however, will not prevent someone or a family from being wiped out through a catastrophic illness.

The last reason for the provision of health care or mandated benefits is the economies of scale in the administration of publicly-provided insurance. The United States has since the 1930's undertaken a system of social security, providing benefits to the disabled and the retired. One of the most outstanding achievements of this system has been the low administrative cost of provision.[16] This compares favorably to the high administrative costs associated with the provision of privately financed health insurance, especially in the case of small groups. Massive savings could occur through the centralization of the government provision or mandating of health benefits.

International Comparisons. There are evidently many reasons for the government intervention in the provision of health care or mandating benefits. It is useful to compare the progress of European countries in their provision of health care and/or insurance versus that of the United States in several important areas.

In most European countries, public assistance or insurance is available to the vast majority of the public. The insurance plans usually allow for all members of society who earn below a certain amount to take part. Table 2.2 lists several examples of European countries and the high percentage of the population covered by public health insurance.

Table 2.2 Percent of Population Eligible for Public Health Insurance, by Type of Coverage: Selected Countries, 1987

Country	Hospital Care	Ambulatory Care	Medical Goods
Austria	99	99	90
France	99	98	92
Germany	92	92	97
Sweden	100	100	100
United Kingdom	100	100	99
United States	40	25	--

Source: Bengt Jönnson, "What Can Americans Learn from Europeans?," in *Health Care Systems in Transition: The Search for Efficiency*, (Paris: OECD, 1990), 88.

As can be seen from Table 2.2, far fewer people are covered under public health insurance in the United States than in Europe. This situation would not be as serious as it is if private insurance picked up the difference. In the United States, as has been previously shown, many people do not have public or private insurance with one of the significant factors being that many of those are employed full-time in small businesses. All this is in the face of the fact that in 1986, the United States paid 10.9 percent of its gross national product on health care versus a European average of 7.2 percent.[17]

Of course, a key question is whether public coverage of large segments of the population will lead to a more healthy population. The World Health Organization lists infant mortality as a good indicator of the overall health of a population, an area where good health care systems can make a telling difference. As can be seen from Table 2.3, of the seven countries listed, the United States has the highest infant mortality (death rates of infants under one year of age per one hundred live births) listed. In fact, of the nineteen European countries listed in the OECD report, *Health Care Systems in Transition*, only Greece and Portugal have higher rates of infant mortality. In the same report, it is listed that Greece spends only 5.3 percent of its gross national product and Portugal 5.5 percent with the United States spending the most of those countries listed with 10.9 percent.[18]

With many pregnant woman uninsured and many families also not covered by any type of insurance, it is little wonder that the United States ranks very low in this key indicator of the health of the general population. This translates into fewer women seeking prenatal care because of lack of insurance. In the U.S. in 1988, the percentage of women receiving prenatal care ranged from the low of 54.9 percent in New Mexico (with Washington, D.C. at next to last at 61.2 percent) to 85.4 percent in Iowa. This directly relates to infant mortality and has led to the nation's capital, Washington, D.C., having the highest infant mortality rate in the United States.[19]

Given the negative effects of those who do not have health insurance and the reasons cited for using health insurance as a means of addressing the market failure that exists in medical markets in the United States and allows anywhere from thirty to sixty million U.S. citizens to go without health coverage, there is a mandate for government to step in and provide a means to allow this large population access to adequate health care. While the poor do have access to

Table 2.3 Infant and Perinatal Mortality Rates: Selected European Countries Selected Years 1970-1986 (Rate per 100 Live Births)

Country	1970	1980	1986
Austria	2.59	1.43	1.03
France	1.82	1.01	.80
Germany	2.34	1.27	.87
Sweden	1.10	.69	.59
United Kingdom	1.85	1.21	.95
United States	2.00	1.26	1.04

Source: Bengt Jönnson, "What Can Americans Learn from Europeans?," in *Health Care Systems in Transition: The Search for Efficiency*, (Paris: OECD, 1990), 91.

some forms of public assistance, the working poor often earn above the minimum levels to allow them access to public health care assistance.

Form of Government Intervention with Given Political Environment

With the assumption that the government should undertake a program to insure that all workers and the poor have access to medical care and are not under the threat of facing large and ruinous medical costs or must refrain from seeking the necessary and optimal medical care because they do not adequately value the benefit of medical services, the question becomes one of how the government should go about providing adequate access to health care insurance.

The two basic choices that the government faces in providing health care coverage are either through the direct provision of health services by government and (funded by tax receipts as is the case in the United Kingdom with the National Health Service), or the mandating of benefits through health insurance provided at the place of work for those employed, with public assistance available to those not working.

One overwhelming argument against attempting to introduce into the United States a system for the comprehensive provision of health benefits or insurance funded through taxes is the budgetary constraints faced by a government that already has a national debt of over three trillion dollars and adds to that debt each year an additional three hundred to 350 billion dollars depending upon whether the funds used to bail out the numerous failing financial intermediaries are included as an addition to the government's debt. An attempt to introduce a program that could cost in the hundreds of billions of dollars a year would have absolutely no political future, whatever the merits.

In addition to the political arguments against using tax revenues to fund a national health insurance, the distortions introduced by any tax are also a reason for not using taxes to correct the market failure. This distortionary effect of taxes, or deadweight loss, occurs because taxes drive a wedge between the actions of people operating in an environment without taxes, as opposed to one with taxes. The waste of resources involved in the search for loopholes and the decrease in the purchase of goods brought on by higher taxes are examples of this wedge. This would be the case in an environment with higher taxes brought on by the need to raise taxes to fund a new national health care system. Thus an additional dollar of taxation could cost society not just a dollar, but substantially more. This deadweight loss has been estimated to range anywhere from $1.07 to $1.33 for each additional dollar of tax, a huge loss to the economy.[20]

The more numerous arguments for a law mandating the coverage of all workers or all citizens below a certain income level (as is in Germany), much as is the case with the national law governing the payment of an hourly minimum wage, include the freedom of companies to design a program for employees that goes beyond the minimum that the law requires. This allows competitive firms to compete for the available labor supply. This benefit to companies would lose some of its significance if the government did away with the tax advantage that business receives when it pays for the health insurance of employees with tax deductible dollars. An employee in return should prefer receiving one dollar of health insurance coverage provided tax free versus one dollar of taxable income of which he is allowed to keep less than one dollar depending on the marginal tax rate he faces.

Employer-financed medical insurance amounted to a decrease in tax revenues to government (a direct subsidy to business to promote employer provided health insurance) of twenty-three billion dollars in 1987.[21] On the other hand, benefits above the minimum mandated benefits eligible for taxation would be taxed at the same rate as a dollar of income. This is an argument for mandated benefits as it could provide additional revenues to government because employees, to be recruited by a firm, would be indifferent as to whether the additional wage used as an inducement was paid in additional medical benefits or in cash. This could lead to additional revenues as the benefit or income is taxed. For instance, as health insurance is mandated in Germany, firms compete by offering more money, thus increasing taxable wages as there are mandated health benefits and employees treat these as a right and benefit of being employed and not as a fringe benefit thrown in by the employer to sweeten the inducement of working at their company.

Both for reasons of efficiency and equity, the market failure leading to the huge number of U.S. citizens without access to health insurance must be solved. The rhetoric that a national health insurance is disguised socialism (all levels of government in the United States contribute more to spending on health care than a "social market" oriented country like Germany) or that the cost of national health insurance would lead to an explosion in spending on health care, are not true. In fact, many studies have shown that a more centralized approach to health care leads to lower costs.[22]

Direct provision of benefits financed through taxes is politically infeasible and leads to deadweight loss. Thus a law mandating benefits could be an answer to the market failure, especially in the case of workers who do not have health insurance, and in light of the fact that in a recent poll, only ten percent of those surveyed would be in favor of a publicly funded health system and fifty-nine percent would favor a system of mandated health insurance.[23]

The next chapter describes the current U.S. health care system in the areas of provision of health care, health insurance and proposals for dealing with the current market failure of the inability of many citizens to gain access to affordable health insurance.

Chapter Two Notes

[1]U.S. Congress Senate. Committee on Labor and Human Resources, *Basic Health Care for All Americans Act*, 101st Congress, (May and June 23, 1989), 91

[2]Adam Smith, *An Inquiry into the Nature and Cause of the Wealth of Nations*, (Oxford: Clarendon Press, 1976), 456.

[3]Kenneth J. Arrow, "Uncertainty and Welfare Economics of Medical Care," *American Economic Review*, (May 1963), 950.

[4]"Doctors, Patients Trade Blame," *USA Today*, (7 May 1991), 9B, 10B.

[5]Milton I. Roemer, *An Introduction to the U.S. Health Care System*, 2nd edition, (New York: Springer Publishing Company, 1986), 114.

[6]U.S. Congress Senate. Committee on Labor and Human Resources, *Basic Health Care for All Americans Act*, 101st Congress, (May and June 23, 1989), 124.

[7]Ibid., 132, 133.

[8]Jeanne T. Black, "Comment on "The Employed Uninsured and the Role of Public Policy," *Inquiry*, (Summer 1986), 210.

[9]Ibid.

[10]Ibid.

[11]Ibid., 211

[12]"You Bet Your Life," *The Economist*, (27 October 1990), 15.

[13]U.S. Congress Senate. Committee on Labor and Human Resources, *Basic Health Care for All Americans Act*, 101st Congress, (May and June 23, 989), 269.

[14] Joseph E. Stiglitz, *Economics of the Public Sector*, 2nd edition, (New York: W. W. Norton & Company, 1988), 299.

[15]"Cutbacks in Health Services Budget Leads to Increase in Measles Cases," CBS Evening News, (15 September 1991).

[16]Joseph E. Stiglitz, *Economics of the Public Sector*, 2nd edition, (New York: W. W. Norton & Company, 1988), 331.

[17]Bengt Jönnson, "What Can Americans Learn from Europeans?" *Health Care Systems in Transition: The Search for Efficiency*, (Paris: OECD, 1990), 89.

[18]Ibid., 90.

[19]"D. C. Ranks Highest for Deaths of Infants in Nationwide Report," from Children Defense Fund Report, *The Stars and Stripes*, (14 August 1991), 5.

[20]Lawrence H. Summers, "Some Simple Economics of Mandated Benefits," *American Economic Review*, (May 1989), 180.

[21]Joseph E. Stiglitz, *Economics of the Public Sector*, 2nd edition, (New York: W. W. Norton & Company, 1988), 285.

[22]A. J. Culyer, "Cost Containment in Europe," *Health Care Systems in Transition: The Search for Efficiency*, (Paris: OECD, 1990), 36.

[23]Eli Ginzberg, "The Restructuring of U.S. Health Care," *Inquiry* (Fall 1985), 280.

CHAPTER THREE

Health Insurance in the United States

The United States has long had a policy of relying on the free market system to provide wide access to a health care system that is the most technologically advanced in the world. Warren Greenberg, in the introduction to the tenth anniversary of an important study on competition in health care, celebrated the increase in competition, which in theory should allow for wide access to affordable health care, while also pointing out that:

> ...competition may have succeeded only in improving the allocation of health resources. In the next ten years, I believe we will have to combine a better allocation of resources with a more equitable distribution of these resources.[1]

Health Care Insurance and Government Intervention

This statement above is not an astonishing conclusion given that among the thirty-seven million U.S. citizens without health insurance, about one-half belong to households with family income below 15,000 dollars with one-third of these being children.[2] Table 3.1 gives a breakdown of the various categories of those insured and not insured. It can be seen that the age groups with the highest percentages of uninsured are the two youngest age groups, while the black and Hispanic categories have very high rates among those without insurance, even Medicaid.

The above comment by Mr. Greenberg is also curious in that the public sector pays for over forty percent of all personal health care in the United States, with the government in the case of Medicare and Medicaid setting the prices of the services for which it pays.

Table 3.1 Insured in the Health Care System in the USA in 1985 by percentage

		Privately Insured	Medicaid Insured	Not Insured
Age	Under 16	70.8%	13.0%	15.5%
	16-24	70.7	7.5	21.4
	25-34	77.5	5.4	16.4
	35-44	83.4	4.1	10. 9
	45-54	81.3	3.7	11.5
Sex	Male	76.6	5.6	14.6
	Female	76.3	8.9	12.0
Race	White	79.6	5.0	12.4
	Black	55.7	21.6	19.3
	Hispanic	55.2	15.9	27.0

Source: Markus Schneider and Jürg H. Sommer, *Gesundheitssysteme im Internationalen Vergleich*, (health systems in international comparison), (Augsburg: BASYS GmbH, 1989), 316.

The system of reimbursement in the United States, both public and private, has led to health care expenditures being the largest as a percentage of gross national product of any country in the world. Even with this being the case, all members of society in the United States are finding that their health benefits, if they exist at all, are being reduced. An examination of the current system will be useful in an attempt to improve its performance in both equity and efficiency.

Public Health Care Insurance

There have been three major movements in the financing of health care in the United States. These are:

1. Increase in insurance coverage after the Second World War
2. Introduction of the Medicare and Medicaid programs
3. Efforts to control costs

Increase in Insurance Coverage after the Second World War

From 1945 to 1960, the number of people with hospital insurance went from thirty-two million to 122 million and the number of physicians' services went from fewer than five million to eighty-three million.[3] This increase is due to the post-war economic boom that lasted well into the late 1960's. During this period, there was a general shortage of workers in the economy as business expanded to meet the demands of domestic demand and European reconstruction. Companies competed for workers through higher wages and better benefits, among which was health care coverage. This period began to end in the early 1970's as the United States entered recession triggered by the first oil supply shocks.

Introduction of the Medicare and Medicaid Programs

The second major event occurred during President Lyndon Johnson's "War on Poverty" and the advent of Medicare and Medicaid. The Medicare program was launched with the passage of Title XVIII of the Social Security Act which was called "Health Insurance for the Aged."

Medicare. Those covered by Medicare are individuals over sixty-five who are eligible for Social Security benefits, disabled individuals and individuals who have endstage renal disease. The largest part of the program deals with the elderly, with coverage broken down into two parts. Under part A, known as hospital insurance, hospitalization and some Skilled Nursing Facility (SNF) coverage are provided. In 1990, Medicare spending was 1.97 percent of gross national product, or approximately 110 billion dollars, which was primarily financed through a 1.45 percent payroll tax on the first 125,000 dollars of income.[4]

Very restrictive coverage is provided under SNF and only for one hundred days. Part A covers ninety days of hospitalization per a certain period of time when a patient is not a bed patient. In addition, each enrollee has a lifetime reserve of 60 days. Under part B, supplementary medical insurance is provided which covers physician services, drugs, X-rays, lab and medical supplies.

Medicare patients pay no premiums for hospital insurance although there is a deductible tied to a per diem cost of care, with this premium rising steadily in the 1980's. The insurance, exclusive of the co-payment and deductible, is funded through the payroll taxes of workers.

The supplementary insurance program is voluntary with premiums and co-payments. The premiums were initially set to cover up to fifty percent of the expenditures of the program, but have decreased to as low as twenty-five percent due to restrictions on premium expenditures with the remainder coming from general public funds.

There is an active market to provide insurance that covers the gap in Medicare's coverage. The insurance will pay for medical expenses and directly reimburse the provider's for beneficiaries' share of their costs.

Medicaid. Another area of government intervention in the provision of health insurance is the Medicaid program for low-income families which is a state-federal partnership. Individual states determine who is covered by Medicaid with individuals covered under the program falling into three categories: (1) cash recipients of the Aid to Families with Dependent Children (AFDC) program; (2) cash recipients of Supplementary Security Income (SSI); the aged, blind, and disabled; (3) the "medically needy," many of whom would not qualify on an income basis, but who have spent a sufficient amount on medical care such that their incomes, net of medical care, fall below certain minimums.

It is at this point that the problem of too few people being eligible for coverage becomes evident. Medicaid generally helps those who live at about one-half of the poverty level, or 5,700 dollars (the official poverty level for a single person in 1988). The Medicaid cut-off in North Carolina was 2,900 dollars. In this example, a person living at the poverty level would have to have 2,800 dollars in medical bills before becoming eligible for Medicaid. For a family of four, the situation is worse. In North Carolina, for example, the annual income-cutoff is 4,600 dollars compared with the federal poverty level of 11,600 dollars. In this example, a family would have to incur 7,000 dollars in medical bills before becoming eligible for Medicaid assistance.

There are some individuals and family members who will never qualify for Medicaid no matter how poor or high their medical bills are. These include any adults under age sixty-five who do not meet the social security definition of disability and who are not caretakers of a dependent-child or pregnant. All these factors combined have led to a decrease in the Medicaid insured population to where only thirty-eight percent of the poor are covered with forty percent of the recent increase in the uninsured coming from the failure of Medicaid to keep pace with inflation.[5]

Benefits under Medicaid include physician services, inpatient and outpatient hospital services, lab services and nursing home services in skilled-nursing homes. States can put limitations on benefits such as the number of inpatient days of coverage, etc. The financing of the program is based on a formula that incorporates state income levels, so that depending on the level of state income, federal contributions go from a minimum of fifty percent to a maximum, in the case of Mississippi, of seventy-five percent. These funds come out of general taxation sources. Initially, federal monies did not have a cap or maximum, however, these have been introduced since the inception of the plan.

There are some major limitations in both Medicare and Medicaid systems, as already pointed out. Medicare's revenues come primarily through payroll deductions which are a certain percentage of income. When payrolls increase, there is an increase in funding for Medicare. When there is a recession and fewer employed workers, Medicare's revenues suffer. With Medicaid, there has been a bias in funding with more and more going to the older recipients of the Medicaid program. For example, in Louisiana, fifty-one percent of Medicaid recipients are children, while only fifteen percent of Medicaid expenditures go to children.[6]

As was pointed out, both with Medicare and Medicaid, a significant hole in the health insurance coverage exists in the area of catastrophic coverage or the large medical bills that can ruin an individual or family. These bills are often left up to another insured group to pay when the original party is unable to pay.

The U.S. Congress tried to tackle this oversight in health care coverage as far as Medicare is concerned with passage of a catastrophic health care bill to help pay for the costs incurred by a long illness and not paid for by Medicare. This bill was passed with much fanfare, but it was repealed after massive protest.

The program had two main weakness. First of all, it did nothing for the general population under sixty-five except tax them. The other fatal flaw was that it let doctors and other agencies decide what should be charged and then they charged Medicare patients whatever they wished in addition to the insurance. An added charge of four dollars a month was coming off social security checks and all persons age sixty-five or older who paid 150 dollars more in income tax per year would be charged a fifteen percent fee up to a maximum of eight hundred dollars. The return on this would be nothing to the poorest as they are covered by Medicaid with the rest usually being covered by a Medigap policy. The benefits of the program were to a few sixty-five and older hospital patients. The program has been repealed and the gap in this health care coverage still exists.

Efforts to Control Costs

It is at this point that the third major movement in health insurance comes into play. Initially, Medicare and Medicaid insurance were under a system where costs to a hospital or other provider were reimbursed for the full costs to that provider for treating patients up to a maximum determined by the charges of all hospitals in the previous year. There were no incentives for providers to operate under these maximum levels. In 1983, the government introduced to Medicare a system that would reward providers to operate under these maximum reimbursement levels. A new system based upon Diagnostic

Related Groups (DRG's), reimbursed a hospital according to predetermined, fixed, payments based primarily on a patient's diagnosis. Providers of care would have to treat a patient's diagnosis. Providers of care would have to treat a patient and receive reimbursement according to a grouping of eighty-three major categories of diagnoses, with these being further subdivided according to surgical procedure and patient age. If treatment was rendered under these fixed charges, the provider kept the difference. If treatment was more expensive, the provider suffered a loss. If the provider accepts the Medicare patient, he accepts the Medicare reasonable reimbursement rate.

Congress also established a national peer-review program, where groups with medical backgrounds were assigned the job of monitoring the appropriateness and quality of Medicare services by reviewing hospital records. Each review group was set up as a private company that hires physicians to evaluate Medicare-related practices. The problems arise because the doctors and hospitals do not want to see their revenues decrease and patients do not want the services received to decrease. In one example in South Carolina, a company called the South Carolina Professional Review Organization took over in a state where only one percent of Medicare admissions were denied payment in a two year period. Immediately after taking over decisions on admissions, forty percent of some hospitals' Medicare billings were denied, compared with a national average of two percent. Hospitals quickly caught on, and by the end of 1987, they had cut Medicare admissions by thirty percent.[7]

Other Forms of Government Supported Health Care Insurance

Given the inadequacies of publicly funded programs such as Medicaid and the prohibitive costs of private insurance, where do people in the United States who are already sick turn to in order to find health insurance to help pay their medical bills? As a partial answer to this question, many states have set up high risk pools to offer insurance to those who are not able to afford the premiums from private insurers because of their belonging to high risk groups. Originating in the 1970's, these pools have been created in twenty-three states and are open to residents (those who usually have lived in a state for six months) who have received at least one and sometimes two rejections from a private carrier.

High risk pools are a last resort to those who cannot otherwise find coverage, but the costs are high. For example, in Illinois, a pool will cost a forty-five-year-old living in Chicago 3,844 dollars a year. This will buy major medical coverage (hospital services, tests, prescription drugs) with a five hundred dollar deductible. This is twice the cost of the most expensive similar individual policy available to people in Chicago.[8] By definition, this will be the case as the pools offer insurance to the "uninsurable," thus leading to adverse selection with only the very medically needy turning to the pools. The pools do achieve savings through combining under one roof the administration of many small populations and reducing the costs of the insured seeking insurance companies willing in insure the poor risk.

Another major drawback of the plans is that they are only able to cover a limited number of people, currently at about 55,000, with many states limiting the number of people they will cover (Illinois can issue only 4,500 policies), with waiting lists standing at approximately one year in duration. These pools usually operate at a loss with the state assessing all state insurers in the state, with some tax relief granted to the insurers to partially compensate them for their participation. The insurance industry is fighting to have states pick up the losses that the funds incur. Given the huge number of uninsured, it is doubtful whether this system can pick up much of the rest of the thirty-six million citizens without health insurance coverage.

Private Health Care Insurance

With public health insurance not able to carry the full load of many citizens, especially the lower-income employed, an examination of the present state of the private health care insurance system would be beneficial in order to ascertain the positive aspects that could be retained in a new system that addresses the market failure that exists.

For Profit Health Care Insurance

Property/casualty insurers in the United States have not been profitable overall in their basic business - insuring risks, in more than a decade. They have been especially hard hit recently by natural disasters such are Hurricane Hugo (four billion dollars) and the San Francisco earthquake (about one billion dollars).[9] In addition, the property/causality insurers have done worse than the Standard and Poors 500 Stock Market Index, with some insurers even going out of business. In the 1980's, four property/casualty insurers went out of business, leaving a likely cost of five billion dollars to be cleaned up by the industry and the states. This could be just the beginning as in the opinion of the National Association of Insurance Commissioners, up to twenty-one percent of insurance companies in 1990 needed regulatory review. This compares to only an eight percent figure in 1978.[10]

Insurance companies take in premiums and invest these to earn interest-income to help pay off any claims. Many of these investments were in junk bonds, or bonds issued by less than investment grade companies. About five billion dollars of junk bonds were defaulted on in 1989.[11] With insurance companies staggering from losses in many areas of their businesses, it is no small wonder that they try to limit their losses in the health care market by only taking on the best risks or charging prohibitively-high prices to cover people.

Weak balance sheets are not the only thing that has insurance companies worried. High premiums have caused two distinct trends - a move to self-insure by business and individuals. In November of 1988, America's biggest insurance market, California, approved Proposition 103, which ordered a twenty percent cut in most property/casualty rates. Although the courts have lessened the impact of the legislation, the industry has taken heed in other lines of insurance as well. The Health Insurance Association of America, which represents two hundred big health insurers, has prepared proposals that would limit rate increases in health insurance and prevent insurers from excluding small business employees with serious ailments. Much of this is to forestall some proposals in the U.S. Congress to mandate benefits.

Nonprofit Health Care Insurance

Individual insurance companies have tried to transform themselves into companies that manage risk instead of bear it. Even the institution that was the last resort for many seeking health insurance, Blue Cross/Blue Shield has become more select as to the risks it will assume. Historically, Blue Cross/Blue Shield plans took on all individuals offering open enrollment policies that anyone could purchase. Currently, only twenty-two percent of the seventy-four Blue Cross/Blue Shield plans offer open enrollment with Blue Cross/Blue Shield evaluating its applicants the same way commercial companies do.

Blue Cross/Blue Shield was founded by organized medicine in the 1930's in order to ensure that hospitals and doctors were paid, and to ensure that the greatest number of individuals had insurance. Given the large number of individuals insured, Blue Cross/Blue Shield could negotiate contracts with hospitals and doctors, winning discounts. They also, as non-profit organizations, were not required to pay federal, and in many cases, state taxes. Initially, Blue Cross/Blue Shield practiced community-rating, with the better risks subsidizing the sick and other high risk groups, thus allowing Blue Cross/Blue Shield to offer relatively lower premiums and coverage. This changed when the commercial insurers started to "skim" the best of the risks away from Blue Cross/Blue Shield by offering lower premiums to members with lower risk. This has forced Blue Cross/Blue Shield, in many cases, to abandon its mission as the insurer of last resort in response to the consumer's search for the cheapest premiums and a mentality of every man for himself.

The leap by many Blue Cross/Blue Shield plans into the fray with the other insurance companies has led to difficulties for many plans. In the fall of 1990, the West Virginia Blue Cross/Blue Shield plan went into receivership, leaving fifty million dollars in unpaid bills. This is the first of forty-three plans to collapse. In total, the plans took in sixty-four billion dollars in premiums in 1990.[12]

Two other large plans in Massachusetts and New Jersey have also run into difficulties, brought on in part by mismanagement, a fact that should not be lost on the people who depend upon them since most states do not view the plans as insurance companies, so they are not covered by state insurance funds in case of a collapse.

Employer Sponsored Health Care Insurance

With the poor unable to depend upon, in most cases, Medicaid, and with the working uninsured not able to depend upon Blue Cross/Blue Shield to provide them access to affordable health insurance, it is becoming increasingly common that the insured workers have not been able to rely upon health insurance plans at work. To rein in increasing health costs, companies have been forcing their employees to increase their share of insurance or treatment costs, join group plans, seek approval of many hospital procedures, and/or require more outpatient versus inpatient care. A big part of the picture is managed care, including Preferred Provider Organizations (PPO's), where groups of doctors and hospitals agree to cut processing costs and fees in exchange for a larger group of patients and certain payment, and Health Maintenance Organizations (HMO's), which offer group specific services for a fixed price. HMO's, however, have run into many difficulties after the signing of contracts. Often, it is not possible to live within the financial terms of agreements because of the inflation of health care costs and mismanagement.

Naturally, employees resist these changes as they usually restrict their choices and reduce their benefits. At Nytex Corporation, a regional company created after the break-up of the telecommunications monopoly AT&T, 60,000 employees went on strike to protest management's demand that they begin paying eight dollars a week towards their health premium cost. The union contends that health benefits were won during union negotiations and these demands to pay health care costs are really benefit cuts.

All citizens in the U.S., whether the poor unemployed, employed and uninsured or employed and insured are facing health care insurance difficulties. The political impact of so many people not satisfied with the current state of health care insurance has not been lost on the U.S. Congress.

Proposed Government Legislation

The most comprehensive attempt to date to try to deal with the problems of U.S. citizens without health care insurance is the bill proposed by U.S. Senator Edward M. Kennedy, Chairman of the Committee on Labor and Human Resources. The plan has two parts. First, the job-based system of health care insurance should be available to all workers in the United States through their employers and second, Medicaid should be expanded to include those not currently covered by Medicaid or job-based insurance.

This proposal is the closest solution to the problem of the uninsured in the United States and will be used as a platform from which to compare and contrast against the successful model of universal mandated health insurance coverage that exists in Germany, a system which takes advantage of the market system in the provision of health services, an integral part of the U.S. health system.

Senator Kennedy points out in his proposal that,

> 46,000 American families are faced with catastrophic health care costs in excess of three thousand dollars that their insurance does not cover...across the country, more and more hospitals are facing a cruel choice between closing their doors to those who cannot pay and closing their doors to everyone.[13]

The first part of the plan, the job-based mandated coverage, will provide health care insurance coverage to twenty-three million U.S. citizens through employer mandated coverage. Firms will be required to provide a basic package of benefits to employees and their families if the employees work a minimum of seventeen and a half hours a week. The benefits include physicians services, hospital services, diagnostic tests, pregnancy and well-baby care and limited mental health care benefits. No exclusions for pre-existing conditions would be allowed and there would be maximum co-payments of twenty percent, deductible of 250 dollars for the individual and five hundred dollars for a family with a maximum on out-of-pocket expenses.

A major concern of business with any type of mandated benefits is that they lose the flexibility of designing a plan to attract workers. Flexibility would be allowed under the plan because the firm would still be able to offer a richer plan to workers should the firm face a tight labor supply market. Employers, however, would not be allowed to cut back on the mandated minimum level of benefits. Small businesses adversely affected by the costs of offering health insurance under the plan would receive a subsidy if the cost of the plan to the business exceeds five percent of gross revenues. This subsidy would equal up to seventy-five percent of the excess costs to the small business.

A cost-efficient proposal of the plan would establish a system of regional insurers in each geographic region where small employers would have access to community rating, group purchasing power and lower administrative costs. Each regional insurer, in order to participate, would be required to offer a standard plan to small businesses that incorporates community-rating (similar to the *Krankenkassen*, or sick funds, system used in Germany and to be discussed in the next chapter).

The proposal to cover the remaining uninsured has as a goal the coverage of all Americans by the year 2000 not covered as an employee. Those between one hundred and seventy-five percent of the poverty line will be covered under identical conditions as those of working citizens. In addition, the plan will cover all deductibles and co-payments of working citizens who are under one hundred percent of the poverty level. The financing of the plan will be the same as under Medicaid, with the federal government matching state contributions.

This plan goes a very long way in covering most of the inequities and inefficiencies discussed in previous chapters, namely the inequity of some workers not being able to afford coverage because of prior conditions and the inefficiencies of those who do not seek medical attention when needed because of the expense associated with the total lack of insurance. It does not deal with the reluctance to seek medical attention because of out-of-pocket expenses associated with co-payments or deductibles. As will be seen in the next chapter, the German system does deal with these concerns as well as contain other attributes in a system that already is working.

Financing the Proposed Health Care Insurance System

The cited impact of the plan includes the benefit of covering all workers with some health insurance, a reduction in hospital insurance costs, a reduction in hospital unreimbursed care costs of 5.2 billion dollars annually, and savings to firms now providing health insurance of four billion dollars. The costs of the plan, as estimated by an independent actuarial firm, will be thirty-three billion dollars, or an average hourly increase to the employer for each employee of sixty-four cents per hour. This thirty-three billion dollars would be offset by the savings experienced by small business and charity care, which as previously mentioned, is picked up by the employers who already have a plan for their employees, thus shifting the cost to firms who hire workers but do not get the bill when their workers become ill, in effect passing the payment on to the larger company that does cover its workers.[14]

Criticism of the Proposed Plan

Those against this plan cite reasons such as the increased burden that will be passed on to the small business and those who doubt the cost projections, instead citing figures such as one hundred billion dollars as the true cost of the program.[15] Insurance companies who see the end of their individual risk-rating schemes are also against the proposal and rightfully so, as they are not allowed to exclude bad risks or terminate coverage once an illness is diagnosed.

The final arbitrator of this dispute should be of course the citizens of the United States. In a poll done by the respected Gallop Organization, the following question was put to 1,014 people:

> Please tell whether you favor or oppose requiring business to provide employees who work 17.5 hours a week or more with a minimum amount of health care insurance, as an alternative to government programs.

Those questioned were given the choice of answering in favor, don't know, or oppose. The results were seventy-three percent, five percent and twenty-two percent respectively. This demonstrates the overwhelming support for such a program as measured by this random sample.[16]

In the current presidential election year, there has been much talk about reform of the health care insurance market (approximately two dozen plans circulating in Congress a year before the presidential election) but there has been no more concrete proposal for reform that the bill introduced by Senator Kennedy. One suggestion by the Heritage Foundation, a conservative think-tank, advocates a system that severs the link between the preferential tax treatment that is given to employers that provide health insurance to their employees. Instead, tax credits would be given to consumers to compensate them for medical costs and the cost of medical insurance which would be necessary to have by law (mandated benefits). The proponents of this plan cite the additional tax revenues that would result from this plan while also solving the problem of the lack of health insurance.[17]

The flaw of this plan is that it does not address the problem of having many providers of health insurance coverage, each competing for the best risk and adding to the total bill the cost of excessive overhead due to the great number of small insurers.

Another plan, proposed by a coalition of business, labor and medical groups, closely follows the Kennedy plan and in addition, proposes a new program called Pro-Health, which incorporates Medicaid and those not covered by insurance. Under this plan, all employers would either provide their employees with a basic health care benefits package or pay a payroll tax of seven percent to Pro-Health in order to cover their employees.[18]

The major flaws associated with this plan are the lack of concentration on removing the consumer from the situation where he must decide the value of medical care, necessitating that he pay large deductibles and out-of-pocket costs, and not recognizing the need to reform the provision of health insurance in the private health insurance markets. The German system of mandated national health insurance provides a means where the consumer does not have to make the decisions on the value of health care, but where cost containment plays an important role.

To this point, the problems associated with the lack of health care insurance coverage and its implications for efficiency and equity have been examined. Given the arguments, based on efficiency and political reality that have also been explained, it appears that the solution to the problem of the uninsured in the United States lies in a system of mandated coverage provided by the independent providers of medical care that already exist, with the coverage sold to the public through a coordinated group of private insurers. The proposal by Senator Edward Kennedy, thus is the most far reaching proposal to address this problem. The primary questions that should be answered is could such a system work. One way to answer this question is to look at a current system that is already in existence with many similarities to the system in the United States. This system is in the Federal Republic of Germany, and the next chapter will examine the successes and the failures of this system to try to gather ideas on what can be successfully applied in the situation in the United States.

Chapter Three Notes

[1]Warren Greenberg, "Introduction to the 10th Anniversary of Competition in Health Care," *Journal of Health, Policy and Law*, (Summer 1988), 223-224.

[2]Deborah Chollet, "The Uninsured in the U.S.," *Employee Benefits Review*, (1988), 3.

[3]Victor Fuchs, *The Health Care Economy*, (Cambridge: Harvard University Press, 1986), 322.

[4]Larry Lipman, "Medicare Reform Needed," reported findings of the Advisory Council on Social Security, *Dayton Daily News*, (16 March 91), 7-C.

[5]U.S. Congress Senate. Committee on Labor and Human Resources, *Basic Health Care for All Americans Act*, 101st Congress, (May and June 23, 1989), 77.

[6]Ibid., 124.

[7]Glen Ruffenach, "Painful Medicine," *The Wall Street Journal*, (31 October 1988), A1, A16.

[8]"The Crises in Health Insurance," *Consumer Reports*, (August 1990), 531.

[9]"Survey of American Insurance," *The Economist* (27 October 1990), 8.

[10]Ibid., 17.

[11]Ibid.

[12]"First Blue Cross Collapse in U.S. Puts Policy Holders in Dire Straits," *The Wall Street Journal*, (12 March 1991), A1, A12.

[13]U.S. Congress Senate. Committee on Labor and Human Resources, *Basic Health Care for All Americans Act*, 101st Congress, (May and June 23, 1989), 3.

[14]Ibid., 11.

[15]Ibid.

[16]Ibid., 25.

[17]Ibid., 36, 37.

[18]"National Health Care Plan Proposed," *The Stars and Stripes*, (14 November 1991), 4.

CHAPTER FOUR

Health Insurance in Germany

Solidarity. This is a key word used in the introduction to a pamphlet produced by one of the largest public health insurance-providers in Germany, one of the many sickness funds. The concept recognizes that when it comes to health insurance, the burden of the individual who becomes ill should be carried by all members of society since all members are subject to becoming ill. The workers should help those who are unemployed, the young should help the old as well as the old caring for the young. Those in training also should have access to health care for they will be in the not too distant future carrying the responsibility for the older and younger generations.

Government Intervention

The German Health care insurance system has evolved for over one hundred years, beginning with the reforms of the health care insurance sector in 1883 by Otto von Bismarck when he created the system of compulsory insurance services and sickness benefits. This was an attempt to bond members of society to the system and it was unique.

During the process of the evolution of the system, the various health care players - patients, doctors, and government, have, while being primarily concerned with their own objectives, created a health care system of checks and balances, where all of the citizens are covered under some health insurance scheme. This is accomplished while spending almost one-third less of its gross domestic product in comparison to the United States and actually decreasing the percentage of gross domestic product devoted to health care over the last decade. As table 4.1 illustrates, Germany was one of three countries among the twenty-five members of the Organization for Economic Cooperation and

Table 4.1 Health Spending by Several Members of the Organization for Economic Cooperation and Development 1980, 1990

Country	1980 (%)	1990 (%)
United States	9.2	12.3
Western Germany	8.4	8.2
Canada	7.7	9.0
Sweden	9.1	8.8
France	7.8	8.4
Ireland	9.8	7.9
Britain	6.0	6.4
Japan	6.2	6.3
OECD Total	6.6	6.8

Source: "Health Spending," *The Economist*, (16 November 1991), 127.

Development (OECD) that accomplished the feat of decreasing health care expenditures as a percentage of gross domestic product during the last decade.

This analysis will concentrate on the evolution and details of the German health care insurance system, giving the details of the mandated coverage system and looking at the relationship between the major players. The goal will be to present the German health care insurance system and highlight those areas that could be applicable to the U.S. health care insurance system.

Mandated Coverage and Sickness Fund

The German health care insurance system is decentralized, with very little direction and financing coming from the federal government and the states. This is in keeping with the sharing of powers between federal and local governments in Germany. The overall coordination of the health care insurance system comes from the *Bundesministerium für Arbeit und Sozial Ordnung*, or the Federal Ministry of Labor and Social Affairs.

All persons under a certain income are by law mandated to have health insurance coverage (deutsche mark (DM) 54,900 in 1989, roughly equal to the average annual compensation in that year). Persons with incomes above that are allowed to be insured under private sickness funds, but they still must have health insurance unless they can put aside a substantial amount which would cover their needs and the needs of their family in case of a serious injury or illness. Those retired and formerly covered under the system, students and persons unemployed, and those working more than eighteen hours a week are also covered. The contributions for the unemployed are made for the first month of unemployment by the former employer and thereafter by the unemployment office. Companies must either contribute to a health insurance fund for their employees or provide the employees with a company-sponsored fund.

Those covered under the mandatory (statutory) health insurance who wish to purchase added benefits such as private rooms, the most qualified surgeons, etc., may purchase such protection from an active market of private health insurance providers. In addition, those above the income limits may option out of the statutory sickness funds in order to decrease their portion of the premiums since, as this is based on a percentage of income, it can become very expensive for those whose earnings rise above the average wage. The private insurers do use experience-rating techniques to screen the applicants for coverage, and the premiums can increase over time so that when one retires and can least afford expensive premiums, the premiums are at the highest. At this point, the retiree will not be allowed back into the statutory sickness fund.

These mandatory insurance plans are governed by the 1,150 different statutory sickness funds or *Gesetzlichen Krankenkassen*. There are many types of sickness funds, including industrial, craft, farmer, government employee, etc. In 1988, twenty-four percent of all sickness funds were small, local funds and they covered forty-six percent of the statutorily enrolled workers.[1] The funds are governed by a board of directors and representatives of employees, so all groups have a say in the administration of the fund. The financing of the funds come primarily from a payroll tax averaging thirteen percent on a base of wages, salaries and pensions, with the employer matching the employees' contribution. Persons with limited monthly incomes (single with deutsche mark 1,260 or married and DM 1,752 with DM 315 for each child) do not have to contribute to the fund.[2]

The financing of the system is made up of 73.5 percent employee/ employer contributions, 11.9 percent public funds, 7.3 percent contributions from the private sickness funds and an additional 7.3 percent made up of personal out of pocket expenses.[3]

The statutory sickness funds are comparable in the services they cover, with these including free ambulatory care and free and unlimited hospital care; freedom to choose any general practitioner or specialist, including dentists acknowledged by the fund; preventive care; family planning; rehabilitative services; maternity benefits to include paid maternity leave of six weeks prior and eight weeks after confinement; and eighty percent of normal wages for those sick up to seventy-eight weeks.[4]

Co-payments have been introduced in recent years in order to decrease the expenditure of the funds and to help the members of the fund realize the economic impact of their use of medical facilities, personnel and medication. The co-payments include a three deutsche mark charge for prescriptions, twenty DM charge for eyeglasses, a fifty percent charge on the material cost of dental work and a ten DM charge per day for hospital stays and the full payment of ordinary travel costs associated with medical treatment. Efforts to introduce co-payments each time a doctor is visited have been unsuccessful.[5]

Physicians Associations

Given that the German system of mandated health care insurance coverage is successful in providing a system that covers the vast majority of its citizens with quality health care at a lower percentage of gross national product that in the United States, it would be beneficial to explore the relationship of the sickness funds in Germany with the physicians, since the physicians are the key to keeping health care costs in check. They are the key because they are the decision makers and would be critical in enabling the introduction of mandated health care insurance in the United States as they are important to the success of the system in Germany.

Part of this success in Germany has been the ability to control the remuneration of physicians. In a study of physicians earning to the average wage in the United States and several other European countries, it was found that physicians net income had not risen as fast as the average national wage and in fact there was some narrowing of the difference. Since 1983, however, Germany is the only country among those surveyed where this narrowing trend has continued. In fact, in the United States, as previously mentioned, from 1981 to 1989, pretax incomes for physicians , after expenses, have risen much faster than the average wage.[7]

This control over physicians incomes is a product of the power that the German sickness funds have because of their size. When the first sickness funds were created, they were given the responsibility of looking out for the health of their members and not just paying their medical bills. This put the funds into a position to start negotiating conditions with physicians. This has led to a system where each side cooperates to provide quality health care at an "affordable" price.

With the passage of the laws which established a compulsory health care insurance scheme and the emphasis on sickness funds to coordinate this task, a natural shift of power happened which gave the sickness funds and their large membership power to negotiate with individual physicians. Fee for service payments were eliminated and doctors were required to treat patients for a fixed price based upon the number of patients. This was, of course, not to the liking of many physicians and there was a strike in 1898 which resulted in the formation of the "Union of German Physicians for the Defense of Their

Economic Interest." This organization gave the physicians power in numbers in order to deal with the sickness funds. After more negotiations at both local and central government levels, it was agreed that physicians would begin serving on the boards of the sickness funds and the sickness funds would contract at local levels with physicians. The physician associations developed into formal groups which are called *Kassenärztliche Vereinigung*, or K.V. (physicians association), and these put an end to the individual negotiations that were going on between the sickness funds and the individual physicians.

Physician Remuneration

The physicians associations evolved into an organization that would receive payments from the sickness funds based on various methods of reimbursement. The most common was a point system where doctors would add up all the points of procedures performed on patients and these would be reimbursed to the doctors from the pool of money given to the physician association by the sickness funds. By the late 1950's, the system had evolved into one where the sickness funds would make quarterly payments to the physician associations based upon the average value of claims in the previous quarter. There was not a fixed budget because it was influenced by the number of claims and services rendered in the quarter. The rates at which the physician associations were reimbursed were negotiated nationally, with variations for regions and category of sickness fund.

Cost Control and Negotiations

During the 1970's, there was an explosion in health care costs. To this point, there had been little federal government involvement in health care financing, allowing it to be handled by the physician associations and sickness funds. The negotiations resulting from the cost explosion left evidence that the players were interested more in their own positions rather than the needs of society.[8] As a result, in 1973, the government created the *Konzentrierte Aktion* or Concerted Action, which was to be an advisory body consisting of government officials, physicians, hospital administrators, private insurance company managers, members of the sickness funds, employers and labor union member. The group is used as a forum to communicate differences and to work toward common goals.

As a result of Concerted Action, a national contract was negotiated between the physician associations and the sickness funds where physicians would be reimbursed based upon a target established from the expenses of the previous quarter. This target would be adjusted for technology, population and morbidity among other things, but for the first time it would take into consideration changes in the average wage rate.[9] In addition, point values were assigned to up to 2,500 procedures , as illustrated for selected procedures in table 4.2. The current rate of reimbursement for each point is ten pfenning (one-tenth of a deutche mark). After the patient is treated, the points are added up and submitted to the sickness fund.

Over the next ten years, it was found that the expenditure target system was not effective in controlling costs. The actual expenditures usually exceeded the target and led to the introduction in 1986 of an expenditure cap at an average of thirteen percent of the employee's wage, shared between employers and employees. In addition, general increases in reimbursement for many funds were not allowed to be greater than the overall wage increases received by the sickness funds' members.

To promote direct patient and physicians contact, separate pools for reimbursement were created with physician consultation services receiving almost fifty percent of the pool of money for reimbursement, lab services ten percent and other services the remainder. This was an attempt to force physicians to rely more on patient consultations and less on testing, in order to put a disincentive on ordering excessive tests. The point values of the services rendered by the physicians are placed in the appropriate pool. Each pool of money is then divided by the total number of points to yield a conversion factor. This determines the rate at which the physicians will be reimbursed, given the total employer and employee contributions in the previous quarter.[10]

The success that has been enjoyed by these efforts to control costs is very positive and can be seen in table 4.3. As can be seen, while the average consumer price index declined by 2.5 percentage points in 1978 - 1987 over the comparison figures from 1970 - 1978, the average change in these five medical cost indices was a decline of 6.47 percentage points. This can also be compared to the overall cost increases experienced in the United States. In the period from 1980 to 1986, the inflation of health care costs was three times higher in the United States as in West Germany while the inflation rate in physician costs was as great as two times as high in the United States as in West Germany. For

Table 4.2 Selected Examples of the Points Assigned to Various Procedures

Procedure	Points
Consultation	80
Consultation and Examination	320
House Call	275
Shot	80
Preparation of a Small Wound	100
Wart Removal	80

Source: Peter H. Herman and Lothar Hanisch, *Gesunheit! Danke, Aber Wer Zahlt* (health! thanks, but who pays?), (Hamburg: Rowohlt, 1988), 66, 68.

the same period, the overall inflation rate in the United States was only one half times that of West Germany, meaning that the rate of increase in health care costs has been much lower in Germany than in the United States over the last several years.[11]

The German system of mandated health insurance is not only successful in providing the vast majority of its citizens with health insurance, but it has also been successful in containing the increase in health care costs in comparison to the United States. This dramatic success of the German health insurance system came about through the joint efforts of all members of the health care system, especially the sickness funds with their huge membership (membership mandatory by law) negotiating through a position of strength with physician associations to reduce the rate of growth of a major factor of health care cost increase, physician incomes.

Efficiency and Consumer Behavior

Given the system of statutory health insurance, it is necessary to investigate the actual mode of consumption of health services. A good question is whether the German health insurance system is more efficient than the one which allows a great number of U.S. citizens to go without any health insurance and had led to an inefficient distribution of health services in a country that spends more on health care, as measured by gross national product, than any other country.

All members of the sickness funds are given vouchers which they can use when they visit a doctor. Instead of paying at the time of receiving the service or receiving a bill later, the patient merely surrenders the voucher at the time of treatment. Services rendered are recorded on the vouchers and these are passed on to the sickness funds by the physicians on a quarterly basis. The patient need only to hand to the care provider one voucher per quarter. This method of payment leads, of course, to a lack of cost-consciousness by the patient since he never actually sees the bill for the services received.

The patient in Germany, it must be assumed, will also be a rational consumer of goods and services and will equate the marginal benefit to the marginal cost of goods and services received, just as the patient in the United States does. Since the patient does not pay any extra for the cost of the services, his actual marginal cost of receiving the medical attention is zero. This will lead

Table 4.3 Average Annual Percentage Change in Indices for W. Germany, 1970 - 1978 and 1978 - 1987

	1970-1978 % Change	1978-1987 % Change
Consumer Price Index	5.6	3.1
Physician Services Price Index	9.0	3.8
Total Ambulatory Care Physician Costs for all Sickness Fund Members	11.3	5.4
Ambulatory Care Physician Costs per Sickness Fund Member Index	11.2	4.5
Cost per Sickness Fund Member per Physician Index	10.7	2.8

Source: Bradford L. Kirkman-Liff, "Physician Payment and Cost Containment Strategies in West Germany: Suggestions for Medicare Reform," *Journal of Health Politics, Policy and Law*, Vol. 15, No. 1, (Spring 1990), 85.

to the consumer using a great deal of medical resources which should show up in increased use of medical services. The patient will not be hesitant to use a service that is free to him, since whether he uses the service or not, he pays his portion of the monthly premium charged by his sickness fund and automatically deducted from his pay. This leads to a higher number of contacts per year with physicians in Germany (10.8) than in the United States (5.4) since most consumers in the United States do see the costs associated with a visit to the doctor in the form of a co-payment or a full payment of the bill.[12] This leads to more self-treatment in the U.S. which does not mean, in all probability, a more efficient use of resources or to lower costs.

In the United States, the patient may be unwilling to consume the extra service for fear of the additional cost. This may lead to a less than desirable use of physicians services which could lead to a delay in seeking needed medical care to the detriment of the patient and perhaps society. This could be persuasive evidence explaining the reasons why the United States spends so much on its health care. In reality, it is namely spending so much treating conditions that could have been handled much more easily and cost effectively if the patient would have seen a physician sooner.

Since most of the cost of prescription drugs are paid for by the sickness funds (recently with the introduction of health care cost reforms, minimal charges have been introduced on the purchase of prescription drugs) here, as with physicians services, there is the possibility that patients will not value at their actual costs the value of prescription drugs, thus leading to more consumption of drugs than necessary. This is supported by the statistic which illustrates that in the former West Germany, medications made up 1.37 percent of gross domestic product while only .73 percent in the United States.[13]

On the other hand, in comparison to several other European countries and Japan, consumers in the United States use, as a percentage of total sales for medications, the most over-the-counter (medications without prescription) medications. This is illustrated in table 4.4 and could be interpreted to mean that consumers in the United States take treatment of illness more often into their own hands. This may be as a result of the hesitancy to consult a doctor given the cost of the visit. If correct, this could be dangerous as shown by a three month long study done by a doctor in Munich, Germany, to ascertain the results of self-treatments of colds and other common ailments. During a three month period, eighteen cases of complicated and life-endangering medical problems

Table 4.4 Over-the-Counter Medication as a Percentage of Total Sales

Country	Percentage
United States	37
Switzerland	30
Sweden	20
Germany	18
United Kingdom	15
Japan	14
France	8

Source: Peter H. Herman and Lothar Hanisch, *Gesunheit! Danke, Aber Wer Zahlt?* (health! thanks, but who pays?), (Hamburg: Rowohlt, 1988), 163.

developed from patients who used over the counter medications instead of seeing a doctor immediately after the appearance of a cold or other symptoms.[14]

Preventive Medicine and Cost Containment

The sickness funds also take the lead in providing preventive care to the members of its funds. Free cancer examinations are provided for those in certain age groups and the larger funds publish monthly magazines that give health tips and provide information in areas such as diet and the safe use of medications. The funds see such services as their obligation to their members and as a method of containing costs. The magazines also attempt to inform the members of the state of finances of the fund to make them aware of the expenditures of the fund.

Another key to cost containment is the control of expenditures on prescription drugs. German doctors who treat sickness fund patients are only allowed to prescribe drugs that are both approved and proven effective. Other drugs will not be payed for by the sickness funds. Those who choose to be treated with the other drugs must pay the difference between the approved drug and the one chosen. Since the cost to the patient will be higher for the drug not on the approved list, in most cases the less expensive drug will be chosen. An effort had been made to place price ceilings on up to eighty percent of all approved drugs. Currently, only thirty percent of approved drugs are on a predetermined price list. Should this goal be achieved, significant price savings should be recognized.

The physician associations also play a key role in containing costs through the economic monitoring of the activities of physicians. This involves comparing doctors in the same specialties with similar patient mixes. Physicians with costs significantly out of line with the average are asked to explain the differences. If the costs are unjustified, the doctor can be excluded from treating sickness fund patients. Representatives from the funds review the results of the monitoring and also make recommendations.

Controlling health care cost-increases through monitoring the decision makers and by discarding the use of experience-rating in determining health insurance coverage and premiums has led to an efficient allocation of resources and the maximum coverage with health insurance of the German population. Cost-containment efforts that have been based on making the patient pay for a larger proportion of health care costs when ill have been predictably unsuccessful. For example, while a co-payment of forty percent for certain dental procedures was initiated recently, dental costs still increased by fifteen percent. In the words of Norbert Blüm, Minister of Labor and Social Affairs and architect of the recent reforms in health care aimed at controlling cost increases, "the recipe of patient co-payments as a means for controlling costs has not lived up to expectations and has lost its magical appeal."[16]

The German health care system of mandated health insurance benefits has been successful in allowing the vast majority of the population to be covered under health insurance and it has done this while controlling rising health care costs. This has been accomplished without major influence being exercised at the federal government level, but through local and regional sickness funds and physician associations. In addition, health reforms have limited the increase in health care expenditures to the current contribution levels of thirteen percent now made on a shared basis between employee and employer, so that increases in expenditures will match increases in worker wages. The system also insures that retirees, the unemployed, those in training and expectant mothers receive adequate health care insurance (including fourteen weeks of paid maternity leave).

The next chapter will deal with devising a new approach to providing all United States citizens with adequate health care through mandated health care insurance. Lessons will be drawn from the German system since it is a system of private physicians similar to that in the United States and because of its success in operating a system of universal health insurance through mandated insurance coverage, an approach which is encompassed in recent proposed legislation by the United States Congress.

Chapter Four Notes

[1]Klaus-Dirk Henke, respondent in, *Health Care Systems in Transition: The Search for Efficiency* (Paris: OECD, 1990), 101.

[2]Markus Schneider and Jürg H. Sommer, *Gesundheitssysteme im Internationalen Vergleich* (health systems in international comparison), (Augsburg: BASYS GmbH, 1989), 144.

[3]Ibid., 146.

[4]Klaus-Dirk Henke, respondent in, *Health Care Systems in Transition: The Search for Efficiency* (Paris: OECD, 1990), 103.

[5]Markus Schneider and Jürg H. Sommer, *Gesundheitssysteme im Internationalen Vergleich* (health systems in international comparison), (Augsburg: BASYS GmbH, 1989), 145.

[6]Simone Sandier, "Health Services Utilization and Physician Income Trends" in, *Health Care Systems in Transition: The Search for Efficiency,* (Paris: OECD, 1990), 50.

[7]Sherry Jacobson, "Doctors, Patients, Trade Blame," *USA Today,* (7 May 1991), 10B.

[8]Paul J. Godt, "Confrontation, Consent and Cooperation: State Strategies and the Health Profession in France, Great Britain and West Germany," *Journal of Health Politics, Policy and Law,* (Winter 1988), 470.

[9]Fritz Beske, "Expenditures and Attempts at Cost Containment Strategies in West Germany," in The Public/Private Mix for Health, (London: Nufield Provincial Hospital Trust, 1987), 251.

[10]Bradford L. Kirkman-Liff, "Physician Payment and Cost Containment Strategies in West Germany: Suggestions for Medicare Reform," Journal of Health Politics, Policy and Law, Vol. 15, No. 1, (Spring 1990), 81.

[11]Markus Schneider and Jürg H. Sommer, *Gesundheitssysteme im Internationalen Vergleich* (health systems in international comparison), (Augsburg: BASYS GmbH, 1989), 396, 397.

[12]Bradford L. Kirkman-Liff, "Physician Payment and Cost Containment Strategies in West Germany: Suggestions for Medicare Reform," *Journal of Health Politics, Policy and Law,* Vol. 15, No. 1, (Spring 1990), 90, 91.

[13]Simone Sandier, "Health Services Utilization and Physician Income Trends" in, *Health Care Systems in Transition: The Search for Efficiency,* (Paris: OECD, 1990), 44.

[14]Peter M. Hermanns and Lothar Hanisch, *Gesundheit! Danke, Aber Wer Zahlt?* (health! thanks, but who pays?), (Hamburg: Rowolt 1988), 167.

[15]Rainer Hupe, *Abkassiert* (cashed in), *Stern*, (14 November 1991), 82.

[16]"Süssmuth Will Arzt-Rechnung für Vericherte," (Süssmuth wants doctor bills for insureds), *Eßlinger Zeitung*, (25 November 1991), 1.

CHAPTER FIVE

A New Health Insurance System

The health care insurance system in the United States need not be abolished to be improved. To the contrary, the framework of the current system provides an excellent basis upon which to build a new system. On the other hand, there is room for major improvements in the system and many lessons can be learned from the last chapter which dealt with the German health insurance system.

This chapter will deal with a proposal to reform the U.S. health care insurance system and it will be broken into four parts:

1. Basic outline of the new system
2. Health care insurance system reform
3. Financing
4. Cost controls

Basic Outline of the New System

The basic premise of the system is that all citizens of the United States should have access to basic health services and to this end, all citizens should have access to affordable health insurance in the form of mandated employer provided health insurance and an expansion of the system to include the unemployed and the poor who do not fall under Medicaid coverage, as was discussed in chapter three.

Health Care for All Americans

A promising start has been made with the Basic Health Care Bill for All Americans that was proposed by the 101st U.S. Congress. As mentioned in chapter three, the plan would mandate that employers provide health care insurance to all their employees. A basic package of benefits would be mandated under the proposal, but the insurer would have the option of expanding coverage to attract employees. The plan would cover all prior conditions and would have employees make co-payments and meet deductibles. To cover the unemployed and the poor who do not fall under Medicaid protection, the Medicaid framework would be expanded under the bill to include all U.S. citizens by the year 2000.

Applications from the German Health Insurance System

As this plan does not go far enough soon enough, a plan based upon the German statutory health insurance system will be proposed to allow both for-profit insurance companies and nonprofit insurance funds to be set up that would cover both the working population and the unemployed to fully take advantage of the pooling of risks that large numbers of insureds can provide. Since it has been estimated that the overhead of insurance companies that provide and administer the health insurance system contributes almost one hundred billion dollars to the cost of the total health bill in the United States, savings just from the pooling of risks can be enormous and would help pay any additional costs associated with including the current uninsured in the system. This does not include the more efficient use of health resources that would occur as consumers take advantage of health benefits at the appropriate times instead of waiting and making uninformed judgements about when health care is needed.

As large companies with health insurance plans for their employees already pay a major portion of the bill for the care of the uninsured through the passing on of these costs to the companies, the savings they would receive through lower health care insurance premiums would also offset much of the cost of insuring those not insured. According to U.S. Senate Majority Leader George J. Mitchell of Maine, the inclusion of the uninsured into a plan which would be financed through employer contributions for their employees would cost the federal government an additional five billion dollars in the first year, but save seventy-eight billion dollars in the first five years of both public and private expenditures.[1]

As shown in chapter three, the German health insurance system pays all costs for most treatments while allowing for co-payments on elective procedures.

In certain respects, this allows for the most efficient outcome in the use of medical resources because patients do not have to make uninformed choices about whether the benefits of necessary procedures are worth the costs, leaving the physician who is in the better position because of knowledge and experience to make this judgement (while placing limits on the physician's ability to increase his income and costs). It also precludes much of the self-treatment that goes on in the United States, as shown by the percentage that over-the-counter medications make up of the total sales of medications.

In the last chapter it was seen that this type of system could lead to an overconsumption of medical services because, as shown by various studies, the price elasticity of hospital care has been estimated to be anywhere from .2 to .7, meaning that an insurance policy covering one hundred percent of health care costs could lead to an increase in demand for health care of anywhere from twenty to seventy percent.[2] In addition, physicians who may have a target income can, given the power they have in deciding on the measures to be used in the diagnosis and treatment of an illness, raise their incomes significantly unless they are monitored. The proposal to be set forth will take these factors into consideration in the design of the new health insurance system.

Government Intervention and Market Economics

The Employed. The primary catalyst to the new system would be a law at the federal level which would require that all citizens have health care insurance and all firms which employ workers would provide their employees with a basic package of health care benefits or pay certain flat tax on wage, salaries and retirement pay which would be for the provision of their employees and retirees with health care insurance.

The actual provision of the insurance would be handled through a mixture of private for-profit insurance companies and nonprofit insurance funds. These insurance companies and funds would only be allowed to compete in areas such as administrative costs and in the additional benefits that they can provide to their members. There would be no competition based upon experience-rating as all competitors would agree to accept all those who apply for coverage, independent of prior or current medical conditions. Employees of firms which do not belong to a Health Maintenance Organization or to a Preferred Provider Organization would be allowed to choose the insurance company or insurance fund to which they would have their firm pay the insurance tax into in order to provide for the insurance coverage.

The Unemployed. Workes who become unemployed would have their share of the insurance premiums deducted from their unemployment benefits with unemployment insurance paying the other half of the premium to allow them and their families to have continued coverage during the prescribed duration of the unemployment benefits. In order to provide coverage for the long-term unemployed, the poor and the disabled, Medicaid would pay the premiums for these insureds instead of, as is now the case, Medicaid paying directly the medical bills of the poor.

Consumer Behavior and Cost Control. Patients under the proposed new health insurance system would be provided with incentives and information concerning the costs of procedures, and doctors would be monitored for their decisions as far as costs are concerned and the success of the procedures ordered. A keystone of the program would be a cap placed on the total amount that employers and employees can pay for insurance. This limit could only be increased when as part of the growth of the economy, additional revenues become available, a system that has led to remarkable cost containment success in Germany under the statutory health care insurance system.

As part of the cost-containment measures that would allow for the implementation of this system, limits would be set on questionable procedures and questionable technologies. Especially targeted would be procedures that expand health care costs but not the life span nor increase the quality of life.

Cooperation. As in Germany, the interests of the different parties in the system would be safeguarded through concerned parties such as the physicians and hospitals forming associations to negotiate with the insurance companies and funds to determine fees for procedures, etc., as is the case with the German system. The federal government would encourage system wide consistent pricing, taking into consideration patient mix and other demographics.

Delivery Systems. The delivery of services would remain unchanged, with hospital ownership remaining a mixture of private and public, with doctors' services provided by predominately independent physicians.

Health Care Insurance System Reform

A health insurance system that is based upon experience-rating will lead, as has been shown in the case of the United States, to a scenario where large segments of the population will go without health insurance coverage. This will occur either because the individual will not pay the premiums given his subjective valuation of the insurance versus the cost, cannot afford the premiums or he is excluded from coverage because he is viewed as having too high of a risk for coverage to be offered by an insurance company that is forced to compete with other companies that are also competing for just the best risks.

Health care insurance companies in the United States have been able to survive by choosing only to insure the population that has the least likelihood of incurring a claim. This is generally the population that needs the insurance the least. It is the segments of society stricken with cancer, diabetes, etc., that need the insurance the most, but they cannot afford the insurance even if it is offered because of the extremely high premiums. Even state sponsored insurance pools for high risk insureds have been unsuccessful because of the resistance of the insurance companies to take on these high risks. The only option left open to the members of society stricken by illness and not insured is to rely upon public and private sources paying the costs associated with the illness through either direct payment of taxpayer monies or through higher hospital bills as hospitals are forced to pass on the uncompensated expenses.

The health care catastrophe that the United States faces through ever increasing health care costs and a growing number of uninsured citizens must be dealt with at the national level and through means that are politically feasible, given the current state of the national debt which exceeds three trillion dollars and is growing by over three hundred billion dollars a year.

Mandatory Health Care Insurance

To meet this challenge, a system of mandated (statutory) health care benefits for all United States citizens is proposed, under which health insurance coverage would be provided to all employees and their families through the employer. This can take the form of an employer sponsored Health Maintenance Organization, Preferred Provider Organization or the contribution, to be matched by employees, to a for-profit insurance company or nonprofit insurance fund, chosen by the employee, to purchase the mandated benefit package.

Under federal guidelines, each state, based upon population and other relevant factors, would allow insurance companies and nonprofit insurance agencies such as Blue Cross/Blue Shield to compete for the pool of insureds. The insurance providing entities would compete entirely on the basis of reducing the costs of administering the payment function between the employers, employees and care provider. A minimum package of benefits would be provided to include ambulatory care and hospital care, preventive care for family planning, maternity benefits, prescriptions, mental health benefits and dental care.

Given that the employee is already contributing to his health care bill through his contribution to his employer, the above benefits would be paid for by the insurance company or entity to the care providers, exclusive of elective procedures. Payments to the care providers would be based upon a negotiated amount (negotiated at the state level) for a certain procedure as is the case under the German health insurance system. Care providers who agree to participate in this system would accept payment from the insurance entity as the complete payment for the service performed. This would not be a new experience to providers of care to Medicare patients under the DRG system. Care providers would be paid on a quarterly basis dependent upon the funds available to the insurance entity given the group of insureds and their contributions and the contributions of their employers. This would lead to limited increases in health care costs which are tied to the growth of the organizations and ultimately to the economy.

Payments to care providers would be segmented into three categories, one for direct physician consultation services, one for laboratory testing, and one for other services. The physician consultation category would have the largest pool in order to encourage patient contact and limit unnecessary testing and other procedures. During the quarter, the total number of procedures provided to the members of the insured group would be totaled and according to the points assigned to each procedure, a result of negotiations between care providers, the insurance entities, and the federal government, the total pool of money would be divided by the total number of points and multiplied by a conversion factor calculated to determine the remuneration to which the care provider would be entitled.

In order to promote competition but limit the number of weak firms to be allowed to provide insurance benefits, the states would accept bids from all qualified insurance companies willing to participate in providing the basic package of benefits to insureds. Insurance companies would submit their bids not in the expectation of gaining the largest share of good risks, but in the expectation of being able to administer the funds placed in their care for the financing of the provision of health benefits and profits would result in their efficiently processing claims and keeping administrative costs to a minimum. The states could promote competition from nonprofit firms by requiring that these firms be allowed to share access to facilities, computers, etc., on a paid time-share basis and by allowing the nonprofit insurance funds to operate without paying federal or state taxes (nonprofit). Insurance companies and funds would compete for customers by not only keeping unnecessary costs to a minimum, but also by promoting preventive health through screenings, education and other programs to minimize the damage to health caused by dangerous activities and habits. By keeping all unnecessary cost to a minimum, the insurance entities would be able to attract more insureds by being able to offer plans richer in services. This is an effort to match the low administrative costs found with public insurance programs, where the costs of administration can be as low as three percent compared to the forty percent faced by many small businesses.

The board of directors of each insurance company and insurance fund would have representatives of both the employers, employees, retirees and care providers in order to represent the interests of each group in the administration and disbursement of the funds collected to finance the provision of medical benefits.

As in Germany, the care provider interest groups would be encouraged to form economic monitoring committees to oversee the practices of providers. The activities of care providers will be categorized into various services given the patient age, sex, etc. The average cost incurred per patient will be compared to the overall group within similar categories, and the care providers whose charges are very different would be asked to explain the differences, and if a board made up of the peers of the provider deem the expenses to be excessive (in Germany, the figure generally used is when the expenses are forty percent or more above average), the provider could be made to pay back part of the charges. Ultimately, excessive charges could lead to the loss of the privilege of treating members of the insurance company or insurance fund.

Under this proposal, all employees of a company, both those active and retired, would be able to participate in this system, with the employer also contributing a fixed percentage to the insurance entities based on the employee's wage or salary or the retiree's retirement pay with contributions from the federal government based on the retiree's benefit eligibility under Medicare. Unemployed workers would be able to maintain membership in the fund while receiving unemployment compensation. The Medicaid program would be expanded to pay the costs for protection for all those not covered by employers, unemployment compensation, Medicare or through their own means.

As in the German health insurance system, patients would be provided with certificates which doctors would accept and on which treatment given to the patient would be recorded. These would then be forwarded to the respective insurance provider. Contrary to the German system, however, insureds would be appraised quarterly of expenditures on their behalf, and if the expenditures are within a certain annual limit (excluding preventive-care and first-time visits), the insurance company or fund would pay more of the cost of elective medical care such as dental work or lower the premium. This would help mitigate the problems associated with overconsumption of medical benefits without discouraging the patient from seeking needed medical attention.

Financing

The various levels of government in the United States currently pay for almost fifty percent of all the nation's health care costs, with the federal government paying thirty percent, state and local governments paying twelve percent and the subsidy that the federal government allows for employers who provide health insurance making up another six percent.[3] This is in contrast to the previously mentioned 11.9 percent of the German health care bill that is paid for through public funds. In reality, the various levels of government in the United States pay a much higher portion of the total health care bill, even though the health system in Germany which is referred to by many in the United States as "socialized" medicine, a term that more appropriately fits the United States if the source of funding is used in that definition. Much of what is spent in the United States is wasted since it goes toward unnecessarily-high administrative costs.

Under a mandated health insurance program as formulated in this proposal, there would be a great deal of consolidation in the health insurance sector and this will lead to great efficiencies as administrative costs are brought from an average of twenty-five percent for small companies today to the five percent levels that the large companies face. This, coupled with increased tax revenues for the federal government as the deduction for providing health care benefits to workers is eliminated, a savings of approximately thirty billion dollars a year, will allow the government to let small businesses, that experience costs in excess of a certain percent of gross revenue (as stipulated in the Bill by the U.S. Congress), to be given a temporary subsidy that would reimburse these businesses for up to seventy-five percent of expenses above five percent.[4]

The Employer-Based Health Insurance

The Basic Health Care Bill for All Americans proposed legislation in Congress places employee contributions to the payment of the premiums for the basic package of benefits at no more than twenty percent of the cost to the employer, with deductibles of 250 dollars for the individual and five hundred dollars for a family. This proposal recommends that a fixed percentage of the employee's pay, salary or retirement pay, to be matched by the employers, be remitted to the insurance companies or nonprofit insurance funds as premiums to pay for the coverage. This contribution by employee and employer would be a reduction compared to the current expenditures on health care benefits for current and former employees.

Small companies have seen their average cost of health care insurance rise from two thousand dollars in 1986 to thirty-two hundred dollars.[5] Large companies have seen their costs soar for corporate employees (given more generous health care plans) to forty-five hundred dollars.[6] Given the proposed five percent contribution from both the employer and employee, the costs for both the small and the large business would be less given an average wage rate of twenty-five thousand dollars per year.

Large companies are especially feeling the burden of their health care insurance bill in light of the new regulation promoted by the Financial Accounting Standards Board in the United States which stipulates that companies must set aside sufficient funds to finance the promised health care benefits to retirees. The funds set aside by the companies will not be able to be written-off as expenses until the actual expense occurs, so these amounts come off the bottom profit line of companies in the United States, and this could total approximately 250 billion dollars, with this amount growing by ten percent per year. This accounting rule change has necessitated that IBM set aside 2.3 billion dollars in earnings in 1990 and General Electric 1.8 billion dollars. Other companies not on as sound a financial footing as these two are putting off making the move. For instance, Chrysler faces a liability of approximately four to six billion dollars with owner's equity of the firm only at four billion dollars.[7] Many firms, given this scenario, would be interested in a program where a certain percentage of the pay of retirees is deducted and turned over to an insurance company in order to finance the health needs of retirees, similar to a defined contribution retirement plan.

As does the Bill in Congress and under the German health insurance system, this proposal recommends that all employees who work a minimum of seventeen-and-a-half hours will be provided with health care insurance. This will allow part-time workers access to health insurance and will take away the incentive for companies to try to keep more part-time employees for the sole purpose of not paying benefits to which full-time employees would be entitled. In addition, this proposal would allow workers who become unemployed to keep health care insurance coverage for themselves and their families for the duration of their unemployment benefits, with their portion of the premiums deducted out of their unemployment insurance with the employer's premium being paid by the state (after, for instance the first month of unemployment).

The Unemployed, the Elderly and the Poor

For the long-term unemployed and the poor, Medicaid would pay the entire premium for the health insurance instead of the situation, as it is now, with Medicaid paying for the medical expenses of the poor, inclusive of the high overhead involved with the monitoring and disbursement of payments. The long term unemployed and the poor would also be able to choose the insurance company or insurance fund that would represent them, and all processing of claims and payments would be handled through the insurance company or insurance fund. This would negate the need for the duplication of this effort by the Medicaid establishment in each state, with significant savings.

Medicare, the program for the coverage of the medical needs of the elderly, would also experience savings from the efficiency of doing away with the duplication that occurs when both private and public entities complete the same tasks. All retirees who are not covered by a retirement plan or whose retirement benefits are insufficient to allow the deduction of the flat percentage rate for the premiums of the health insurance coverage, will be covered under Medicare. This will eventually decrease the fiscal responsibilities of Medicare as the burden of caring for the elderly portion of the population is paid for by both current workers and from the retirement pay of former workers. This would negate the necessity of building reserves under the current social security system to cover the medical needs of retirees and lead to decreases in payroll taxes associated with the Medicare program expenditures, a tax now at 1.45 percent of earnings.

Cost Control

As the concerned parties have discovered with mandated health benefits in Germany, in order to contain costs, a cap must be placed on expenditures of the health system. This cap would be based upon the total contributions made by all participants to the health insurance system through the flat percentage paid on wages, salaries and retirement earnings of retirees with contributions from Medicare and Medicaid. As stated previously, health care providers must divide the proceeds of this pool among themselves based upon the services provided. If too many services are provided for the full amount of the negotiated compensation for the services to be paid, a percentage of the total would be paid to the care provider, and the care provider in order to remain in the system must accept this as full compensation.

Monitoring groups set up by the individual categories of care providers would be used to monitor the practices of the members to ensure that none are far above normal in the cost of care delivered. Those who are far out of line with the average would be required to explain the differences, and if these explanations are not adequate, the health care provider could be made to pay back part of the excess or even prevented from further treatment of the patients of the insurance company or fund in the respective state. This pool of funds could not be increased unless the wages that the contributions are based upon also increase, a sign that a growing economy could afford more health care.

This system of a cap being placed on expenditure had led to a superior performance in the containment of costs in Germany through the 1980's, with increases adjusted for inflation far below those seen in the 1970's and below those seen in the United States, also adjusted for inflation.

Cost-Containment Through Cooperation and Other Means

The emphasis of this system is cooperation between employers, employees, retirees, care providers and government. All participating parties realize that it is in their own interests to safeguard the interests of all members of the system and not just to pursue their own agenda. As in the case with the group responsible for promoting cooperation in the German health insurance system, Concerted Action, so too will it be necessary to foster cooperation that enables improvements in the entire system that will benefit all participants.

While the expenditure cap will go a long way in controlling the health care costs in the entire economy, other steps must be taken to aid this cost containment effort. To this end, all participants will be interested in concentrating resources as efficiently as possible, and this will require emphasis on treatments and technologies that are effective both in healing patients and containing costs. For instance, a methodology must be employed in evaluating treatments as to this trade-off. For example, Alan Maynard of York University in England, had formulated a concept called the Quality Adjusted Life Years (QALYS), which ranks treatment cost, the age and sex of the patient and outcome. For example, artificial hips are high on the list because the increase in the quality of life versus the cost is very high while heart transplants are rated relatively low. Systems such as these give some guidelines as to how health care resources can be allocated.[8]

Questionable procedures that do not prolong life or make it more livable, will also come under scrutiny. For instance in a 1988 study, it was concluded that removing tissue from the prostate gland after the appearance of non-cancerous growth does not prolong life, but this procedure costs Medicare about a billion dollars a year. In addition, each year in the United States, sixty out of every one hundred thousand people have a coronary bypass, in Britain it is only six out of the same number. Are the differences valid? For instance, a study found that performing cervical smear tests on women every three years yields ninety-five percent as much benefit to the early detection of cancer with only one-third the cost of the usual annual tests.[9] The emphasis on this movement is on outcomes and a heavy emphasis is on prevention. Doctors would be fully reimbursed for preventive procedures with less than full payment for others. More emphasis on cleaning up environmental pollutions, more screenings in order to promote early detection, vaccination and incentives for changing damaging behaviors of individuals would all lead to decreased costs and better health. Performing procedures that are cost effective would be part of this.

It would also be in the interest of those financing the health care system to limit investment in technologies that produce questionable returns on the investment. The insurance system can have a powerful influence on whether technologies are developed. For example, in the late 1980's research on a cochlear implant for the hearing impaired was discontinued after the introduction of the DRG system because the qualities that the new technology would bestow on the hearing impaired were not deemed to be an improvement great enough to warrant the increase in cost that would have made the development cost worthwhile.[10]

The purchase of an excessive number of medical devices can also be discouraged. In some cases, excess has led to the absurd. For instance, in Los Angeles County, with a population of seven million, there are more computerized tomography (CT) scanners than there are in all of Great Britain with a population of fifty-five million.[11]

A look at containing costs in the U.S. health care environment would not be complete without something being said about malpractice suits. Given the lack of coordination between the interested parties in the health care market decisions over what constitutes appropriate medical care and compensation for injury caused by "negligence" have been left up to the judicial system.

Both the number and size of malpractice suits have increased dramatically in recent years. For instance, between 1979 and 1983, the number of lawsuits per one hundred physicians doubled (tripled for obstetricians/gynecologists). The average medical malpractice verdict increased from 423,000 dollars in 1975 to more that two million dollars in 1986.[12]

The awards have pushed up the cost of malpractice insurance in recent years to doctors and this increase has been passed on to consumers. Many states have tried to limit the awards in the areas of intangibles such as mental anguish, but with limited success. For instance, in the state of Florida in 1988, an attempt was made to limit other than actual tangible damages to one hundred thousand dollars, but this was defeated by the lawyer lobby. In order to arrest this increase in malpractice suits and awards, a more concerted effort must be made to show the damage that these cause in both increased premiums through the payment of awards and through care providers ordering more tests than needed in order to document every possibility, without regard to its cost effectiveness. Table 5.1 illustrates the extreme increases in malpractice insurance premium rates. In one year 1985-86, the insurance premiums for physicians in obstetrics/gynecology increased 97.4 percent. One often cited estimate of the cost of defensive medicine to protect oneself from litigation, i.e. excessive tests, etc., is put at 10.7 billion dollars in a recent year.[13] A concerted effort would be more likely under a system that encourages cooperation, as opposed to confrontation, as the system under this proposal does.

The ability of the insurance companies and insurance funds to act in the interests of the insureds will be a key to the success of this proposal. In Germany, the sickness funds have been successful for this reason as they are viewed as acting in the insured's interest, without excessive intervention from government. It is a cooperative effort to provide the entire public with health care insurance and access to health care benefits while both using society's resources as efficiently as possible and harnessing the power of the care providers, insurance entities, employers and employees to act using the strength of the market mechanism to allow consumers of medical goods the widest selection at the lowest price.

A summary of the proposed health care insurance system can be seen on the last two pages of this chapter.

Table 5.1 Average Yearly Increase in Malpractice Premium Rates for Basic Limits Coverage by Specialty (Percent), 1982-1987

Year	General Practice	General Surgery	Obstectrics/ Gynecology
1982-1983	17.4	11.0	30.0
1983-1984	22.6	19.3	19.1
1984-1985	26.7	14.3	23.7
1985-1986	85.9	72.7	97.4
1986-1987	27.3	27.2	27.9

Source: Patricia M. Danson, "Liability for Medical Malpractice," from survey data in HCFA Survey of Malpractice Insurance Premiums, *Journal of Economic Perspectives*, (Summer 1991), 60.

PROPOSAL OUTLINE

I. Government Intervention

A. All U.S. citizens to have health insurance with mandated employer coverage of employees

II. Health Care Insurance Mandated Benefits

A. Mandated coverage of services including preventive care, ambulatory care, inpatient care, prescription drugs, maternity care, mental health, and limited dental care

B. Deductibles and co-payments limited to elective procedures

C. Upon requesting treatment from care providers, insureds would present vouchers from insurance funds

D. Care providers would record services rendered on vouchers and these would be forwarded on a quarterly basis to insurance funds

E. Quarterly statements sent to insureds informing them of benefits used with incentives for optimal usage of resources

III. Insurance Funds

A. Competition at the state level between several for-profit and nonprofit insurance funds

B. Insurance funds would compete for the premiums of insureds offering enhanced services through lower administrative costs

C. Insurance funds would not be allowed to deny coverage based upon experience-rating practices

D. Insurance funds would collect premiums for insureds and pay care providers on a quarterly basis negotiated amounts for treatment performed

IV. Financing

A. Employers and employees to split the cost of premiums, which will be set at a cap of ten percent of gross wages, salaries and retirement pay

B. Employers to have the option of establishing HMO's, PPO's, etc. or offering enhanced benefits

C. Short-term unemployed will have premiums paid for out of unemployment compensation

D. The poor, disabled and elderly will have their portion of the premiums paid for by Medicaid and Medicare

E. Care providers, after negotiation with the state insurance funds, will be obligated to accept the quarterly payments as full payment of services

V. Cost-Containment and Cooperation

A. Administrative savings from elimination of experience-rating

B. Savings through optimal allocation and use of health care resources

C. Emphasis on prevention, cooperation and effective treatment

D. Encouragement of cooperation between insurance funds and care providers (i.e. physician associations) with members of each group serving on the board of the other, monitoring of activities of members, etc.

E. Limitation on malpractice lawsuits

CHAPTER FIVE NOTES

[1]Elliot Carlson, "Dems Unveil Health Plan," *AARP Bulletin*, (July, August 1991), 1,3.

[2]Joseph E. Steglitz, *Economics of the Public Sector*, second edition, (New York: W.W. Norton & Company, 1988), 286.

[3]Eli Ginzberg, "The Restructuring of U.S. Health Care," *Inquiry*, (Fall 1985), 273.

[4]Joseph E. Steglitz, *Economics of the Public Sector*, second edition, (New York: W.W. Norton & Company, 1988), 285.

[5]Susan B. Garland, "A Prescription for Reform," *Business Week*, (7 October 1991), 84.

[6]"Soaring Medical Costs: New Number, Same Story," *Business Week*, (28 October 1991), 10.

[7]"Pensioners' Health Benefits: Counting the Cost," *The Economist*, (12 October 1991), 100, 102.

[8]"Health Care Survey," *The Economist*, (6 July 1991), 21.

[9]"The Future of Medicine," The Economist, (20 October 1990), 21, 22.

[10]Burton A. Weisbrod, "The Health Care Quadrilemma," *The Journal of Economic Literature*, Vol. XXIX, (June 1991), 538.

[11]Milton I. Roemer, *An Introduction to the U.S. Health Care System*, second edition, (New York: Springer Publishing Company, 1986), 114.

[12]Joseph E. Steglitz, *Economics of the Public Sector*, second edition, (New York: W.W. Norton & Company, 1988), 294.

[13] Patricia M. Danzon, "Liability for Medican Malpractice," *Journal of Economic Perspectives*, Vol. 5, No. 3, (Summer 1991), 54.

CONCLUSION

With an approaching presidential election and with the economy in recession, many more citizens of the United States are joining the ranks of the unemployed or those fearing unemployment. This means that many will lose one of the prized benefits of employment in the United States, namely affordable health care insurance.

As the number of unemployed and uninsured grows, so too will grow the pressure on the federal government to address the problem of this prohibitively-expensive or unobtainable (because of prior medical condition) good that has been left up to the forces of the market to provide to United States citizens. All other industrialized countries have systems in place that guarantee their citizens health care insurance, looking upon coverage as a right and not a benefit. It can be only a matter of time before it becomes a right in the United States.

In the preceding pages, economic analysis has been used to clearly illustrate that market forces cannot be depended upon to ensure that U.S. citizens will have access to health care insurance. Competitive market forces cannot be depended upon to work when both the supply of the good (medical care) is in the hands of self-interested and organized providers and the demand for the good is in the hands of uninformed consumers. Medical goods cannot be compared to markets for apples and oranges, where the consumer can make an informed judgement as to the benefit received in comparison to the costs. If Mr. Mendez fails to make the correct judgement concerning the severity of the illness of his child (a relatively high probability given his lack of medical training and knowledge), then the consequences will be at best a worsening of the condition of the child and higher medical bills, a situation that cannot be equated with efficiency.

The reliance upon the consumer to be the force which determines the amount of medical care to be consumed does not take into consideration his limited knowledge nor the role of the care provider in determining which tests will be conducted and what treatments will be administered. In other words, making the consumer bear more of the cost of treatment through co-payments and deductibles will lead to an underusage of necessary medical care and will not decrease costs (it may even lead to increased costs) as the care provider is the main driving force in increased expenditures on health care.

Given the inability of the market to provide millions of United States citizens with health care insurance (market failure) and given that the power of the consumer cannot be used to control the increases in the amount of gross national product that is devoted to health care, then clearly there is a place for government intervention in the market. After determining the existence of the market failure, the reasons for it and the inefficiency which results, the remainder of this analysis deals with exploring the form of intervention that should take place.

The federal government of the United States already plays a major role in the financing of health care through the Medicare and Medicaid programs and through the tax subsidy business receives when it provides health care insurance to its employees. This massive intervention in what is seen to be a competitive market is much greater than the amount of funding that the federal government of the Federal Republic of Germany provides to the funding of its health care system, even though, given its system of statutory health care insurance coverage and mandated employer provided benefits, it is viewed as having a more "socialized" system of health care.

In fact, however, the health care system in the Federal Republic of Germany relies upon a system of primarily private health care providers which work in close cooperation with the sickness funds, which represent the interests of insureds. While it is mandatory that all citizens have health care insurance coverage, the federal government provides relatively little of the financing of the health care system. The majority of the financing comes from employers, who are required to either provide insurance coverage to their employees or contribute to one of the sickness funds for their employees, and employee contributions.

In the area of cost-containment, the German health care system has enjoyed tremendous success in the decade of the 1980's (actually decreasing the amount of gross domestic product devoted to health care), in stark contrast to the performance of the health care system in the United States during the same period. Much of this success is directly related to the system of statutory health insurance and employee mandated benefits. Given the pressures of German reunification, it is not surprising that health care expenditures have risen given the new demands of the population of the eastern part of the country. The current system, however, should prove the best able to accommodate these new pressures.

Since the United States finds itself in times of forced fiscal austerity, a system of providing health insurance coverage for all citizens without having to resort to increased taxes, while still drawing upon the resources of a primarily private network of care providers, looks attractive. Parts of the German health insurance system are applicable to the system in the United States and accommodate the strengths of the current system while improving upon the weak areas.

The health care insurance system proposed here is based upon mandating health care insurance benefits and taking advantage of the current medical infrastructure. The next steps to be taken will be at the national level of politics. This analysis should provide the core of a plan that will allow for both the equitable and efficient use of health care resources.

APPENDIX

A.1 International Comparison of the Number of Physicians per 1,000 Citizens

A.2 International Comparison of the Number of Hospital Beds per 1,000 Citizens

A.3 International Comparison of the Number of Hospital Personnel per Bed

A.4 International Comparison of the Price Index for Health Care, Total

A.5 International Comparison of the Price Index for Physician Care

A.1 Number of Physicians per 1,000 Citizens

Country	1975	1986
Canada	1.72	2.07
Great Britain	1.11	1.35
Sweden	1.72	2.77
Germany	1.89	2.70
U.S.A.	1.70	2.22

Source: Markus Schneider, Jürg H. Sommer, *Gesundheitssysteme im Internationalen Vergleich* (health systems in international comparison), Augsburg: BASYS, 1989, 379.

A.2 Hospital Beds per 1,000 Citizens

Country	1975	1985
Canada	-	6.72
Great Britain	8.84	7.44
Sweden	14.31	13.66
Germany	11.80	11.06
United States	6.79	5.48

Source: Markus Schneider, Jürg H. Sommer, *Gesundheitssysteme im Internationalen Vergleich* (health systems in international comparison), Augsburg: BASYS, 1989, 388.

A.3 Number of Hospital Personnel per Bed

Country	1975	1985
Canada	-	2.16
Great Britain	1.18	1.71
Sweden	-	1.80
Germany	.97	1.20
United States	2.06	2.77

Source: Markus Schneider, Jürg H. Sommer, *Gesundheitssysteme im Internationalen Vergleich* (health systems in international comparison), Augsburg: BASYS, 1989, 390.

A.4 Price Index for Health Care, Total.

Country	1975	1986
	Index 1980 - 100	
Canada	64.8	147.5
Great Britain	50.1	149.5
Sweden	61.4	157.8
Germany	78.9	119.7
United States	63.4	163.0

Source: Markus Schneider, Jürg H. Sommer, *Gesundheitssysteme im Internationalen Vergleich* (health systems in international comparison), Augsburg: BASYS, 1989, 396.

A.5 Price Index for Physician Care

Country	1975	1986
	Index 1980 - 100	
Canada	67.22	-
Great Britain	-	-
Sweden	60.2	-
Germany	76.0	119.0
United States	62.9	148.1

Source: Markus Schneider, Jürg H. Sommer, *Gesundheitssysteme im Internationalen Vergleich* (health systems in international comparison), Augsburg: BASYS, 1989, 397.

SELECTED BIBLIOGRAPHY

Anderson, Kevin. "Health Spending Pumps USA with Jobs, Growth." *USA Today*, 7 May 1991, 10B.

Beske, Fritz. "Expenditures and Attempts at Cost Containment in the Statutory Health Insurance System of the Federal Republic of Germany." *The Public/Private Mix for Health*, London: Nufield Provincial Hospital Trust, 1987.

Black, Jeanne T. "Comment on 'The Employed Uninsured and the Role of Public Policy,'" *Inquiry*, Vol. 23, Summer 1986, 209-212.

Bovbjerg, Randall R. "Insuring the Uninsured Through Private Action." *Inquiry*, Vol. 23, Winter 1986, 403-418.

Carlson, Elliot. "Dems Unveil Health Plan." *AARP Bulletin*, Vol. 32, No. 7, July-August 1991, 1, 8.

Chernick, Howard A. and Martin R. Holmer. "Tax Policy Toward Health Insurance and the Demand for Medical Services." *Journal of Health Economics*, 6, 1987, 1-25.

"Chrysler Proposes Novel Health Plan." *The Stars and Stripes*, 22 July 1990, 3.

Cleeton, David L. "The Medical Uninsured: A Case of Market Failure?" *Public Finance Quarterly*, Vol. 17, No. 1, January 1989, 55-83.

"The Crisis in Health Care." *Consumer Reports*, August 1990, 533-549.

Culyer, A. J. "Cost Containment in Europe." *Health Care Systems in Transition: The Search for Efficiency*. OECD Social Policy Studies, No. 7, Paris: OECD 1990, 29-39.

"Cutbacks in Health Service Funding Leads to Increase in Measle Cases." *CBS Evening News*, 15 September 1991.

Danzon, Patricia M. "Liability for Medical Malpractice." *Journal of Economic Perspectives*, Vol. 5, No. 3, Summer 1991, 51-69.

"D.C. Ranks Highest for Deaths of Infants in Nationwide Report." *The Stars and Stripes*, 14 August 1991, 4.

Ellis, Randall P. and Thomas G. McGuire. "Insurance Principles and the Design of Prospective Payment Systems." *Journal of Health Economics*, 7, 1988, 215-237.

Evans, Robert G. "Tension, Compression, and Shear: Directions Stresses and Outcomes of Health Care Cost Control." *Journal of Health Politics, Policy and Law*, Vol. 15, No. 1, Spring 1990, 101-129.

Fuchs, Victor R. *The Health Economy.* Cambridge: Harvard University Press, 1986.

"The Future of Medicine: Warning - Doctors Can Damage Your Health." *The Economist*, 20 October 1990, 21-24.

Garland, Susan B. "A Prescription for Reform." *Business Week*, 7 October 1991, 82-86.

Ginzberg, Eli. "The Restructuring of U.S. Health Care." Inquiry, Vol. 22, Fall 1985, 272-281.

Godt, Paul J. "Confrontation, Consent and Cooperation: State Strategies and the Health Profession in France, Great Britain and West Germany." *Journal of Health Politics, Policy and Law*, Vol. 12, No. 3, Winter 1987, 459-480.

"Groups Say U.S. Must Act to Control Health Care Costs." *The Stars and Stripes*, 2 November 1990, 2.

Hermans, Peter M. and Lothar Hanisch. *Gesundheit! Danke, Aber Wer Zahlt?* (health! thanks, but who pays?). Hamburg: Rohwohlt, 1988.

Hess, John L. "The Catastrophic Health Care Fiasco." *The Nation*, 21 May 1990, 698-701.

Hupe, Rainer. "*Abkassiert*" (cashed in). *Stern*, 14 November 1991, 80-86.

Jacobs, Phillip. *The Economics of Health and Medical Care*. Maryland: Aspen Publishers, 1987.

Jacobson, Sherry. "Doctors, Patients, Trade Blame." *USA Today*, 7 May 1991, 9B, 10B.

Jönsson, Bengt. "Cost Containment in Europe." *Health Care Systems in Transitions: The Search for Efficiency*. OECD Social Policy Studies, No. 7, Paris: OECD 1990, 87-104.

Kern, Rosemary Gibson and Susan R. Windham. *Medicaid and Other Experiments in State Health Policy*. Washington, D.C.: American Enterprise Institute for Public Policy Research, 1986.

Kirkman-Liff, Bradford L. "Physician Payment and Cost Containment Strategies in West Germany: Suggestions for Medicare Reform." *Journal of Health Politics, Policy and Law*, Vol. 15, No. 1, Spring 1990, 69-97.

Lalli, Frank. "There's a Doctor in the House." *Money*, July 1991, 5.

Leader, Shelah and Marilyn Moon, editors. *Changing America's Health Care System*. Washington D.C.: American Association of Retired Persons, 1989.

Lipman, Larry. "Medicare Reform Needed, Panel Says," report from the Advisory Council on Social Security. *Dayton Daily News*, 16 March 1991, 9-C.

Maynard, Alan. *Health Care in the European Community*. Pittsburgh: University of Pittsburgh Press, 1975.

"Minority Health Care." *USA Today*, 31 July 1991, 8.

Morone, James A. "American Political Culture and the Search for Lessons from Abroad." *Journal of Health Politics, Policy and Law*, Vol. 15, No. 1, Spring 1990, 129-143.

National Health Care Reform. Washington, D.C.: AFL-CIO, 1990.

Navarro, Vicente. "A National Health Program is Necessary." *Challenge*, May-June 1989, 36-40.

Organization for Economic Cooperation and Development. *Financing and Delivering Health Care: A Comparative Analysis of OECD Countries*. OECD Social Policy Studies, No. 4, Paris: OECD, 1987.

Pensioners' Health Benefits: Counting the Cost. *The Economist*, October 12, 1991, 100, 102.

Pfaff, Martin. "Differences in Health Care Spending Across Countries: Statistical Evidence." *Journal of Health Politics, Policy and Law*, Vol. 15, No. 1, Spring 1990, 1-28.

Price, Tom. "Uninsured Risk Health Care for All, Panel Told," report on testimony before the U.S. Congress Finance Committee's Subcommittee on Health for Families and the Uninsured. *Dayton Daily News*, 24 July 1990, 12-B.

Pullian, Susan. "First Blue Cross Collapse in U.S. Puts Policyholders in Dire Straits." *The Wall Street Journal*, 12 March 1991, 11, 12.

Reinhardt, Uwe E. "Economists in Health Care: Saviors, or Elephants in a Porcelain Shop?" *The American Economic Review*, Vol. 79, No. 2, May 1989, 337-342.

Regula, Ralph. "National Policy and the Medically Uninsured." *Inquiry*, Vol. 24, Spring 1987, 48-56.

Roemer, Milton. *An Introduction to the U.S. Health Care System*, 2ND ed. New York: Springer Publishing Company, 1986.

Ruffenack, Glen. "Painful Medicine." *The Wall Street Journal*, 13 October 1988, A1, A16.

Sandier, Simone. "Cost Containment in Europe." *Health Care Systems in Transition: The Search for Efficiency.* OECD Social Policy Studies, No. 7, Paris: OECD 1990, 41-51.

Saywell, Robert M. and Terrell W. Zollinger. "Hospital and Patient Characteristics of Uncompensated Hospital Care: Policy Implications." *Journal of Health Politics, Policy and Law*, Vol. 14, No. 2, Summer 1989, 287-307.

Schneider, Markus and Jürg H. Sommer. *Gesundheitssysteme im Internationalen Vergleich* (health systems in international comparison). Augsburg: BASYS GmbH, 1989.

Smith, Adam. *An Inquiry into the Nature and Causes of the Wealth of Nations*, Oxford: Clarendon Press, 1976.

"Soaring Medical Costs: New Numbers, Same Story." *Business Week*, 28 October 1991, 10.

Stiglitz, Joseph. *Economics of the Public Sector.* New York: W.W. Norton & Company, 1988.

Summers, Lawrence H. "Some Simple Economics of Mandated Benefits." *The American Economic Review*, Vol. 79, No. 2, May 1989, 177-183.

"Survey American Insurance: The Trick is to Stay Upright." *The Economist*, 27 October 1990, 6-20.

"Survey Health Care: A Spreading Sickness." *The Economist*, 6 July 1991, 3-22.

"*Süssmuth Will Arzt-Rechnung für Versicherte*" (Süssmuth wants doctor's bill for insureds), *Eßlinger Zeitung*, 25 November 1991, 1.

U.S. Congress. Senate, Committee on Labor and Human Resources, *Basic Health Benefits for All Americans Act: Hearings before the Committee on Labor and Human Resources*, 101st Cong., 1st Sess., 1 May and 23 June, 1989.

Weissbrod, Burton A. "The Health Care Quadrilemma: An Essay on Technological Change, Insurance, Quality of Care and Cost Containment." *Journal of Economic Literature*, Vol. 29, No. 2, June 1991, 523-552.

"Worrying About Health." *The Economist*, 15 June 1991, 47-48.

Zinn, Laura. "Ouch! The Squeeze on Your Health Benefits." *Business Week*, 20 November 1989, 110-122.

INDEX